WHO'S THE DADDY

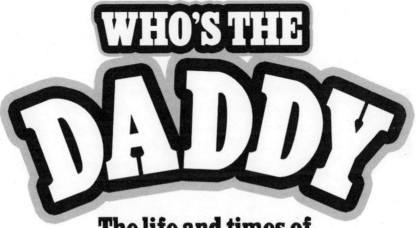

WHO'S THE DADDY

The life and times of Shirley Crabtree

RYAN DANES

pitch

Pitch Publishing
A2 Yeoman Gate
Yeoman Way
Durrington
BN13 3QZ
www.pitchpublishing.co.uk

A CIP catalogue record is available for this book from
the British Library

ISBN 978-1-90917-860-1

Typesetting and origination by Pitch Publishing.
Printed and bound by CPI Group (UK) Ltd, Croydon, CR0 4YY

Contents

This book is dedicated to Sjt
Christopher John Reed (6 rifles)
11 April 1983–1 January 2009

Acknowledgements

To my wife Vicky for your patience, my children Talliah and Seraya, Shirley's daughter Jane Wade, to Paul Dann for the writing space, and to all of my family and friends.

And also: Peter Thompson, Tarzan Darren, Banger Walsh, Rob Cope, Russell Plummer, Mick McManus, Bob Sweeney, Ace Allcard, Ray Robinson, Sid Askin, John Lister, Max Crabtree, Lonnie Cook, Mike Lacey, Ken Sowden, Greg Lambert, Tony Scarlo, Sam Betts, Brian Dixon, Farmer John Allen, Rob Wallser, Dave Dowling, Kevin Phillips, Chris Rutter, and John Chambers, to name but a few…

"There have been pretenders, and there have been contenders, but only one king. My dad."

Jane Wade (February 2013)

The New London Theatre, Wednesday 7 March 1979

THE SHOW began with serious trumpeting. A fanfare of some importance and the audience were applauding. It felt like history was being made, although some of the people there that night, figures dotted throughout the whole of Shirley Crabtree's life, would later think differently. Once the limelight faded there would be a divided opinion on the Crabtree clan and their influence on professional wrestling, and we shall come to these matters in due course. For now, we are trying to conjure up a scene, resurrect a bit of telly history so to speak, so we're looking down at the TV cameras, which are themselves trained on the mock-auditorium set up at the front. There is empty raised seating either side of the doors centre-stage, and a backdrop of red, brown, and cream. Every set of eyes is focused on the doors and over all of this, the shows superimposed titles come and go.

Although the audience were familiar with people like Kent Walton and Dickie Davies on *World of Sport* on Saturday afternoons, there was a certain amount of excitement on their faces as they waited for a different kind of show to begin. This was a live recording and their unblinking eyes shining back through the fag smoke could mean only a couple of things. They were either totally transfixed as they clapped like brainwashed seals, or they'd had a skinful in the Prince of Wales on Drury Lane before the show. How many times they had seen these opening sequences on their televisions at home, and now they were here witnessing it for themselves. And then it all went flat for a couple of seconds as the applause continued. They were waiting for something to happen, anything to happen, which would justify coming out in the dark and missing *Crossroads*.

> *"This is your life; this is Eamonn Andrews and for the next few minutes, I am the hooded monster or words there about, and my intention is to gate-crash a studio-call, a photo-call for grapplers and wrestlers which is taking place in the London room, which is part of this building. So I've got to get there in time to get close to somebody, the sort of Daddy of the grunt and groan business, but to get in and get close to him, I need some camouflage, and my camouflage takes the shape of three sporting gentlemen…"*

Gorgeous George was next to appear. Dressed all in black he looked like Danny La Rue and was camper than a row of pink tents. He wafted on to the stage and waved to the crowd like he was the Queen of Sheba, and maybe that was how he managed the masked wrestler in his charge, the one some called the most controversial in the business. Out-foxing the fox, out-gimmicking the gimmick, may have been the only way he could keep a lid on the "Oriental Master" Kendo Nagasaki whose fury was relentless. Of course, all of this made one hell of a ringside show and George continued to manage Kendo's affairs until he died in 1990.

And what of the self-proclaimed mystic himself? Kendo was the third man through the doors and by then Eamonn was heading off of the stage. Besides this, he probably didn't give a monkeys about the man behind the mask, although he did know the business a bit. Eamonn had been an amateur Irish boxing champion as a kid, so he had more than a passing interest in the wrestling. He was also the original presenter of *World Of Sport* when it started on TV in 1965, but the chances are he probably didn't have a clue about Kendo's "supernatural powers", and the jovial Dubliner soldiered on until 1987, when he died of heart failure at the relatively young age of 64. Whether Kendo Nagasaki was the most powerful man to come from Stoke-on-Trent remains to be seen as Bruno Brookes and Robbie Williams were also born in the city. He was certainly the best at dressing up and his flair for hypnotism and his ability to see the future put him right up there with people like Russell Grant and Mystic Meg. Real name Peter Thornley; he was born in 1942, and he made his wrestling debut in Walsall at Willenhall baths in November 1964 wearing a mask and tight-fitting pants. The fact that the baths were only 122 miles away from the Orient (who had themselves enjoyed some time in the limelight when they reached the FA Cup semi-finals in 1978) probably had no significance whatsoever, although Kendo can be credited with doing the "Martial Arts" gimmick a good few years before Bruce Lee entered any dragons.

Entering dragons was something the fourth man definitely wasn't scared of. By the time 40-stone Giant Haystacks appeared wearing what looked like the armless remains of his mum's sheepskin coat, Eamonn had given the big man the thumbs-up and was leading George and Kendo into the audience. Off stage the only light came from a blue neon sign above a flight of stairs, which read *This Is Your Life,* and some of those scurrying out of the theatre at the end of the night to catch the last bus really didn't need a reminder. Britain in the late 1970s was pretty bloody bleak if you were skint, and characters from the wrestling provided light relief, whether you were watching them on TV, over a couple of pints down the Legion, or you had paid your £1.50 to go see one of the 4,500 yearly shows.

Haystacks lumbered along behind the others like a stray silverback, his dark eyes glaring out through his fur. Real name Martin Ruane; he had once been part of a successful tag team when Shirley returned to wrestling in the early 1970s. It was however, the Big Daddy versus Giant Haystacks grudge matches in the latter part of the 1970s and 1980s which topped the bill right across the land. Despite the lack of proper wrestling and their limited technical ability, the audience's enjoyment of their theatrics was not affected. The powerhouse bell-butts and holds they performed showed a good amount of agility for big men, and besides this, they were the ones who put the most "arses on seats". Halls and stadiums everywhere were packed to bursting point as were their leotards and costumes.

Martin was born in Camberwell, London, in October 1946 and was a big lad who started out as a labourer and a doorman at the weekends to earn extra money to feed his family. He worked at some of the less reputable nightclubs in Salford, Manchester, until he nearly became the victim of a drive-by shooting one night while working the door. Originally taking up wrestling in 1967 as Luke McMasters, it was as Giant Haystacks, fighting Big Daddy on TV on Saturday afternoons that left such an impression on people's minds, and through these bouts both men's statuses have been elevated as the years have passed.

Looking back, the young wrestling fan of today would find it difficult to see the entertainment value in two fat blokes bumping into each other in the ring. Over-exposed to the steroid-fuelled 21st-century American brand of wrestling supermen, comparing British wrestling to its Yankee cousin is a bit like comparing Butlins to Disney World. These were care-free days before ram-raiding and PlayStations became popular teenage pastimes, and kids were easier to impress. It was an age of innocence when creatures lived on Wimbledon Common, and the TV wrestlers were kings. Today, it would be as tough to explain how exciting these bouts were as it would be to explain the beauty we once saw in jumpsuits, Crimplene trousers, and the Bay City Rollers. How supercharged the audience became at the sight of a pair of man-boobs, or the outline of a scrotum in the half-light above the canvas, would be hard to explain unless you had experienced it for yourself.

The London room was dark and filled with wrestlers, and Big Daddy stood in the centre of them all in a white leotard. At a little over 6ft 2in, the 26-stone star was well past his fighting prime and was only too aware that the Big Daddy image was what the people wanted; the wrestling came second. The fact that his brother Max had become the biggest promoter in the land, and turned him into an unbeatable champion, infuriated many of the other wrestlers in the business. They felt good wrestlers were kept back because of the Daddy machine but some of those that were good enough did get their break in America when the British scene died. Love him or hate him, wrestling was experiencing a downturn, and Max Crabtree breathed new life into it when he was made the boss of Joint Promotions, and the televised shows ran for nearly 20 more years. Whether he could have been as successful and kept as much control by promoting others like he pushed his brother is unlikely, and this did not become a real problem until Shirley approached 60 years old, and the plug was pulled on British wrestling on television.

Traditional opinions about Max having total control over his brother's successes are unkind to Shirley and a number of people around him who helped create his John Bull-like character. With a mop of blonde hair under a silver or gold sequined top hat, he would come to the ring in his shimmering cape encouraging the audience to chant "easy, easy, easy". With the Seekers' hit 'We Shall Not Be Moved' blaring away you knew, deep down, that he wasn't going to be bloody well moved, but still you watched on until that last Daddy-splashdown.

It is perhaps correct to say that Max put Shirley up on to a pedestal with his efforts as a promoter, but once he was up there; he had to stay there. The success of the Big Daddy character beyond wrestling and into the wider media was more to do with Shirley, his wife Eunice, and a few people close to them. In the wrestling world, Max didn't trust anybody to run his kingdom and not take a bite, so he made his brother unbeatable. People came to watch him in their thousands because they wanted to see

Big Daddy before they watched any wrestling – it was as simple as that.

The London room fell silent, and the photographer motioned for the group to look into the camera. Shirley was stood in the middle of a burly group of wrestlers wearing his white leotard; still unsuspecting. They all shouted out their lines as the scene cuts to Haystacks shuffling along like he had soiled himself and Kendo behind him bringing up the rear. From the right, another cameraman swoops in as Eamonn (still masked) appears from the opposite side with the red book and microphone hidden beneath his cape. Waving it under Shirley's nose the colour drains instantly from his face as Eamonn removes his headgear, and he says: "Star of wrestling, the big daddy of them all, known to millions as Big Daddy, tonight this is your life!"

Chapter One

A Boy Named Shirley

"How many times I'd picked myself up off the ground after getting a pasting in the early days I can't remember. Shirley Temple was the name they teased me with at school, and I can still recall one time, in particular, when a group of lads set upon me. I got shoved around the centre of a circle, and they were pushing with proper hatred. I could see it in their eyes; they loved every minute of it.

"Do you remember the Johnny Cash song? 'A Boy Named Sue'? The father calls his son Sue because he knows he won't be around to protect him as he grows up, and the lad has to learn to fight because he's constantly battling those who want to take the mickey out of his name? Well, that song described me down to a tee now I look to the past and think about it, and after a while I started to get very angry. The desire to defend myself became overwhelming and the bullies' days were numbered because I hit back twice as hard."

By ten years old Shirley was a bit bigger than most lads the same age and the nastiness was starting to become a bit of a permanent fixture, as was the absence of his father. The name he shared with him was a burden in more than one way because nobody had seen

17

him in two years, and at the time his mother was pregnant with his brother Brian so it hit home hard.

Shirley became a bit of a loner who tried to stay out of the rough and tumble as much as possible. You were more likely to see him with his head buried in a newspaper or a book than giving somebody a knuckle sandwich around the back of the Anderson shelter. The three Crabtree boys were brought up in complete poverty, and Halifax's industry spewed its pollution out onto the grimy streets all the time so fresh air was in short supply. Despite all the hardship, there was still no reason for lowering standards, and their mother wouldn't have any trouble or swearing from any of them. Later, she didn't like to see her boys drinking or smoking, which is something that stayed with them all their lives.

Shirley senior walked out on his family a bit before the start of the Second World War. He had been a rugby player and a wrestler as well as a drayman, and he lived most of his days in Halifax where he was born in 1906. Some people believe the name Shirley came from the Charlotte Bronte novel of the same name, coming from the wild and windy moorland which inspired her to write it in 1849. Before then, the name Shirley was a boys' name but granny Crabtree liked it so much that she gave it to her son, who carried it on. Whatever the truth, it was a cruel name to bestow upon a lad in 1930, and leaves you wondering whether the dray-man had been sampling his own brew the day his wife gave birth to her first child (who weighed in at a couple of pounds under a stone).

In his day, Shirley senior had been a very good professional rugby league player and was part of Halifax's 1931 Challenge Cup-winning side. This would have put the family on a bit of a high with a few quid extra when young Shirley was taking his first steps, but they were never what you would call affluent. He went on to play over 100 matches for the club before winding up his career with York and then Dewsbury. As a wrestler, he experienced a second sporting peak in the 1940s and was described as a "decent amateur" but he was considerably smaller than his son even before the dramatic weight increase and the beginning of the Big Daddy gimmick.

*"My roots are not so much in places, as in people...
From the time I was seven, my childhood was pretty
tough, that's when our old man left us. His differences
were all with my mother... He'd had dumbbells
made for me and my two younger brothers Max and
Brian, had a little mat in front of the fire, and taught
us to hand-balance and wrestle... When he went
my brothers and me made a little gym of our own
excluding him. We had a mat from straw and canvas
and had broom handles with flat-irons on them...
His whole existence was based on his great strength,
he learnt his living by it... He'd go round bars and
clubs doing a strongman act, bending bars and lifting
people up. We grew up fighting fit and soon had the
advantage over other lads. He would encourage us to
join in the street fights to bring out our competitive
element. He'd get us to go up to big chaps and pull
them along the street. It sounds ridiculous, but we had
to do it. He thought that being tough and winning was
the only thing that mattered in life.*

*"He believed in being the hard man and not giving
anybody else a break. He undoubtedly left his mark on
Max and me.*

*"He was unstable [Shirley's father], a bit of a
romantic really. If he had a bit of success, he would
immediately think he could do absolutely anything
and, of course, he'd find that he could not. Typical, I
remember the day he went to a local fair, and they had
a greasy pole with a side of ham at the top. Everybody
had been trying to get up there all day, but it was my
father, by practically busting a gut, who reached it.
And he immediately thought, as usual, that meant he*

could do anything he set his mind to. It was my mother who had to calm him down.

"When he took off it was our mam who worked in the mill twelve hours to keep a roof over our heads and pay the bills. Suddenly, I was the man of the house; we lived at number five Wilson Street where I was born on the 14th November 1930. The house was your typical mill-worker's two up, two down with no piped water and the Armitage Shanks was down the other end of the yard which caused all sorts of problems when it rained.

"My mam's name was Marion, and she was one hell of a woman I can tell you. She weighed 15 stone; her dad was a blacksmith, and she used to strike the hammer. She had tremendous arms on her; she could carry a hundred weight of coal up six flights of stairs… The way she just carried on when dad left, she had staying power and was as hard as hell and her influence on me and my brothers shouldn't be underestimated. All her working life she was up at five every morning to start her shift at the mill and would sometimes come home very late. Despite all of this, and the fact we had a house-trained rabbit that liked to eat the wallpaper, the house was always spotlessly clean, and we were expected to do our bit."

Wilson Street and the surrounding neighbourhoods were regarded as slum areas, and there were no state benefits then either. If you didn't graft, were bone idle, or a drunk, you went under – it was as easy as that. These were the days of the Great Depression when most people's priority was to put food on the table and avoid stuff like unclean drinking water and tuberculosis. If you couldn't pay your rent at the end of the week, you would find yourself out on the street and your kids would end up in the workhouse more than likely.

It was a complete lack of anything with sub-standard housing this was proper squalor, and it got ten times worse when the Second World War started and rationing began. The only thing good to come out of it all was the fact that a lot of other lads didn't have their fathers at home either, they were off fighting, so Shirley suddenly found people who had the same thing in common as him. And of course, there was always the chance the old man would find his way back home, get kicked out by whoever it was he was shacked up with, or his credit would run out.

There was a feeling of doom and gloom in the air at Christmas 1939 and hardly any of the usual seasonal merriment. It was more a season of caution where people didn't want to let their guard down because careless talk cost lives. The Palace picture house was still open though, and films like *The Wizard of Oz* and *Come on George!* provided an escape from the blackout and bad news which was largely about the battles going on in the Atlantic.

Locally, a chap called Arnold Binns decided the time had come and he strapped himself into a pair of his best roller skates and blew the John o'Groats to Land's End record away. There had been a textile strike in the town around the time of Shirley's birth but when the fighting started a few years later such political and social events ceased as people banded together and focused on surviving. There were still things to do, but it all ended when it got dark and people stayed indoors. The war had been rumbling along for three months when Halifax really started to be affected, the world was suddenly changing at a frightening pace, and the people of Britain wondered what was going to happen to them. It truly hit home in November when a single bomb lit up the night sky with smoke and flame and destroyed the West Hill pub and a row of adjacent houses. Shirley and Max were old enough to pick up on what was going on, and it was a frightening time for young lads growing up among it all. A major producer of cotton and wool, Halifax mobilised itself to play its part in the war effort.

There had been a case of mass hysteria in the town the year before when it was believed the "Halifax Slasher" was on the prowl. Scotland Yard was called in; businesses were temporarily shut down, and crazed groups of vigilantes roamed the streets beating up suspects. It all turned out to be a tissue of lies, and the people involved were charged with public mischief offences. One of the men who said he was attacked admitted he had inflicted the injuries upon himself, but the damage was done and an uneasy, paranoiac feeling that the "Bogey Man" was out there on the moors watching settled in the psyche for a time. Soon, that paranoia became real fear as bombs rained down from the skies, and Yorkshire got hit really hard.

To make things worse it was freezing outside as the country experienced one of the coldest winters in many years. The Salvation Army were concerned about families living on the breadline, so they went around the town giving out presents and food, and the Crabtrees qualified. Max and toddler Brian were delighted with their gifts of Meccano, a train set, and toy soldiers, but Shirley wasn't so pleased. After the old girl had dropped her collection tin and warmed her legs over the scattering of coal in their grate, she pulled out a lovely dolly for big sister Shirley, and he never lived it down.

Shirley's schooling started at Pellon Lane Junior in the mid-1930s with a lad called Jack Wilkinson, who went on to win the Rugby League World Cup with England, as well as representing Great Britain as a prop. The two men stayed in contact until they were in their 20s but lost touch as they pursued individual careers. They finally caught up on *This Is Your Life* in 1979 where the only story old Jack could recall after all of that time was one about a linen handkerchief Shirley's mum used to pin to his jacket, so he could wipe his chops after lunch.

It was during those formative years at Pellon Lane that the wrestling education began. He had started out practising holds on the rug at home with his dad when he was still around, and now it was on the school timetable which seems rather bizarre looking at it from today's point of view. What you have to remember is before the scripted displays of showmanship overtook the need for proper wrestling (and the Big Daddy gimmick was a major part of this change) there was a very serious element to it all even though it wasn't quite considered a sport. Put it this way, you would never see a bookie offering odds on a wrestling bout unless he had gone daft, but it was a massive part of the British psyche for most of the 20th century and was on terrestrial TV for 33 years.

> *"Sometimes you look back at it all and you don't know how we managed. It was just me, my brothers and my mam and I remember the beginning of the war very well. I was still having problems in the school yard, and I was getting sick of it. This particular day I got as mad as hell, so I stood up tall and retaliated. I hit the lad squarely on the jaw, and he went down like a sack of taties. I can vaguely remember the schoolmaster bellowing at me to come back but there was no way I was taking any more punishment, and I ran quicker than the day we got caught pinching apples and the farmer's Alsatian had the arse out of my trousers."*

With a keen interest in English literature the library was where Shirley retreated a lot of the time, and it was better than messing about in the street. It was among the sports books and magazines that he first came across a picture of the world-famous strongman Eugene Sandow, and it left quite an impression. Eugene is widely regarded as the father of modern bodybuilding who came from Prussia in 1885 and travelled Europe as a circus athlete. People marvelled at his muscular physique, although the common belief back then was that bodybuilding made a man cumbersome, rather than enhancing his strength and conditioning. Eugene started performing on the London stage in 1889 and was earning big money. Hardly anyone in the professional sports world was training with weights, and Sandow's methods inspired many people, although bodybuilding did not become really popular in Britain until the 1950s.

Eugene started and ran his own fitness magazine as well as creating an institute for physical culture. He was the 19th-century equivalent of Arnold Schwarzenegger making appearances in films by the Lumiere brothers, although they were not quite action-packed thrillers. Back in 1894 audiences still thought cinematography was the work of the devil, and they were freaked out by the trees swaying in the background so they weren't really interested in Eugene flexing his muscles in the foreground.

With the days of bullying behind him and the teenage hormones kicking in, Shirley saw weightlifting as a decent way to get fit as well as impress the girls. Without a father figure, he needed somebody or something to aspire to and the image of Eugene stayed with him as he started to lay the foundations for what lay ahead. It was to be a career of two halves, in the 1950s as a serious wrestler winning British and European belts, and a comeback in the 1970s as the unstoppable showman Big Daddy when he was past his prime. When we look back at those performances now, from the muscular Shirley Crabtree of the 1950s, through several wrestling pseudonyms to the larger-than-life public character, the fights of Daddy and his contemporaries seem so rough, ready and dated they once again enthralled. There were of course those fighters that could sell it and others who were terrible at working the crowd. It was an era of hard-men, hustlers and egomaniacs, all ducking and diving in and out of Victorian music-halls with walls held together by nicotine and spit. Shirley became a star in the places he had first visited as an awestruck boy, and he packed them to the rafters year after year.

Wrestling was experiencing one of its peaks during Shirley's childhood, and the three brothers marvelled at well-known grapplers such as Francis St Clair Gregory, Jack Pye, and Bill Garnon. It was first introduced to the public as a variety act at the beginning of the 19th century to enhance boring strongman attractions. The truth is, once you had seen somebody bend a few nails, lift a couple of bar bells, and hold cannons as they were fired, there wasn't a great deal of action to be had. If you suddenly found yourself heading out of the freak show on Whitechapel Road on a wet and windy winter's evening, and you didn't fancy Soho, you would be looking for a different kind of action to take your mind off what you had seen.

Poor old Joseph Merrick was one of the attractions at the time, and you would need a stiff drink and a bit of light entertainment after seeing the hideous deformities of the "elephant man". Into this kind of environment wrestling was born, the fairground and carnival booths were where the hardmen, and not-so-hard-men, usually fought until they were covered in blood. Sometimes it was done for money, other times to settle a grudge, but out of these places, wrestling gradually evolved to a professional standard. The strongman and bodybuilder shows grew ever more popular and through such men "grappling" and showing off their strength and physique it is easy to see how wrestling slipped into the public consciousness. It was only natural that people would want to see such colossuses beating ten bells out of each other, so the first proper promotional partnership was formed by Sir Atholl Oakeley and Henry Irslinger to help wrestlers hurt and maim each other in a more civilised manner.

Oakeley and Irslinger built upon the developmental work done by Charles B. Cochran, who encouraged legitimate champion Georg Hackenschmidt to go for showmanship rather than sportsmanship because he was wiping the floor with everyone he fought. Born in Estonia in 1877, Georg was the first freestyle champion of the world and spent most of his life in London where he was nicknamed the "Russian Lion". His invincibility was killing the sport so entertaining the crowd became the number-one priority for Hackenschmidt and other top wrestlers rather than a legitimate sporting victory. This of course sowed the seeds for the variety act which evolved over the next couple of decades, and because of the things these wrestlers did to one another nobody doubted its authenticity.

There was still legitimate wrestling going on. Fighters such as Cornish-American Jack Carkeek challenged people in the audience at fairgrounds and carnivals to last ten minutes with him in the ring. Francis St Clair Gregory (another Cornishman) travelled to France to represent his county in the Cornu-Breton tournaments in the 1930s and won all seven of the contests. Men like Jack Dale, Bert Assirati, Les Kellett and George de Relwyskow all started out in the 1930s, and all of these men went on to shape the business in various ways.

Before the First World War, a lot of the big names were leaving to wrestle in America and taking their gimmickry with them. It was there that Hackenschmidt lost his three-year-old world heavyweight title to Iowa-born Frank Gotch in a straight contest which lasted two hours. While Britain suffered under war-time constraints, wrestling continued as a legitimate sport until Oakeley and Irslinger came along. They had seen for themselves how popular "showmanship" wrestling was, and they introduced it properly to Britain in the form of vicious contests that they claimed were real. The new style was called "all-in wrestling" and there were up-and-coming stars such as Tommy Mann, Black Butcher Johnson, College Boy and Atholl Oakeley, who won a series of matches and crowned himself the first British heavyweight champion. Many regard these as the halcyon days of British wrestling; little did they know it was all about to be disrupted by a megalomaniac dictator with a passion for genocide and knee-high boots as Shirley recalled:

> *"Halifax was hit hard by the Blitz, maybe not as badly as Sheffield or Bradford with its steel and industry, but it got its fair share, I can tell you. The sound of a bomb going off is something you will never forget, and you lived in fear of this, although I suppose you did become used to it after a while; you had to cope or you would have cracked up. Most of the houses in town are great big stone structures, and ours had a basement. I remember one night when the sirens were going off our mam was in bed, I ran upstairs and shouted 'quick,*

*let's get down to the basement', but she wasn't budging.
She was so knackered after a long shift at the mill, and
she told me to leave her alone, if she was going to die
anywhere it would be in her bed – what will be, will be."*

The Crabtrees were a pretty normal Roman Catholic family
who kept themselves to themselves, which is something else that
stayed with Shirley later in life. As Big Daddy, the media interest
surrounding him could be intense, and an intrusion for a man
who liked his privacy outside the glare of the spotlights. By the
early 1940s, he had moved on to Battinson Road School as people
just carried on with things. It was difficult because one day you
could be chatting to friends in the town, and the next morning
they could all be dead and their neat little house with its white
picket fence was now a smouldering hole in the ground. The
reality of it was that the country was on its knees fighting for its
very existence until something happened that would change the
course of the war. On the morning of 7 December 1941 the US
naval base at Pearl Harbor, Hawaii was attacked by the Japanese
and nine ships were destroyed, and almost 2,500 people killed as
the United States' hand was forced. Back home, things had been
pretty bleak as Britain stood alone against Germany.

With the Americans now involved, there was a new sense of
optimism, and soon Hitler's forces would weaken as the tides of
fortune began to turn. By the time Shirley's teenage years began
in November 1943, the RAF had started their bombing campaign
on Berlin, and the Allied advance continued into Italy. Fortunate
to be just a couple of years too young for conscription in wartime,
some of his friends' older brothers received their papers before
hostilities ceased, and they saw the devastation for themselves.

For the Crabtrees, things continued much the same as they had
before and Shirley's interest in health and fitness came to the fore.
As well as wrestling he started to play rugby league for the school
and was quick to notice the similarities between the two. He was
good enough to play for Halifax Youth, but he excelled at other

"physical sports" such as shot-put and bench-pressing, and all of this information helps us to build up a picture of an athletic young man. Despite the hardships of war and family life, he came out of childhood relatively unscathed but there were others that weren't quite so lucky. More bombs fell on Bradford, Leeds and Wakefield before the blitz of Sheffield in December 1940 left 660 people dead and 1,500 injured, and there was still more to come.

In 1944, aged 14, Shirley left school, and he immediately helped to take some of the burden off of his mother by getting a job at a spinning mill where he towered over all the ladies like a giant. One of his party tricks was to lift one of them up over the wall to see if the boss was coming, and if he was they would put out their fags and make it look like they were working. Shirley's job was to replace the bobbins on the sewing machines, and he was very happy to be away from school and earning money. Overseas, Operation Overlord was completed in August, and Paris liberated, as the fear of German invasion began to fade. Shirley began to train at the YMCA gym in Halifax where a man called Norman Morrell spotted his potential and encouraged him to wrestle, but he did not think of fighting as a way to make money at that point. With his blonde hair and baby face a very willing Shirley listened to what those around him had to say and his keenness (coupled to the fact that he had a smattering or two of skill and charisma) was enough to get him his big break once he had mastered the trade.

In 1945, Bert Assirati became the British heavyweight champion, and he held on to the title for five years. These were troubled times, the "all-in" style of wrestling was collapsing just like Hitler's empire and Morrell realised that something had to be done. Elsewhere, top wrestler Ted Beresford, who had organised army wrestling contests throughout the war, got involved with Morrell and other prominent men to sort it all out, which left promoters outside the cartel excluded. By agreeing to rotate the talent the new Joint Promotions was soon running 40 shows a week and there was a need for wrestlers who could offer something a bit different. Shirley was still a few years away from being involved in all of this, but he was happy to be around Morrell and his associates while it was coming together, and Morrell was not the only one who regarded him as one for the future.

He was fortunate to receive some training from the "Russian Lion" himself – Georg Hackenschmidt, who was approaching 70 years old, as well as Norman Walsh, Jack Procter, Bernard Murray and Les Kellett during those early years, and regularly trained morning, afternoon, and at night. Not only did they teach Shirley about wrestling and weight training; he picked up tips on diet and nutrition although his insatiable thirst for milk probably came from Hackenschmidt, who was reported to drink up to 11 pints a day.

Norman Morrell became a top wrestling promoter, but he started out as a very good amateur wrestler who was chosen to represent Britain in the 1936 Olympic Games. He went on to become a professional but by the end of the war, he knew that wrestling was crying out for a major overhaul, people were abandoning it because it had become such a farce. Adapted from the American style, Morrell penned a new set of rules, which formed the basis of wrestling for half a century to follow. He did this by persuading former Antarctic explorer Lord Mount-Evans, Commander Archibald Campbell, and MP Maurice Webb to put their names to the "Admiral Lord Mount-Evans rules" which then gave him enough clout to make them stick and they did many things like set up meetings between members of the House of Lords and the promoters as Shirley remembered:

> *"The days of bloody out of the ring fighting, and mud-bath wrestling were numbered as gimmickry was firmly slapped back into its place. People started calling it a load of old rubbish, and commenting on its authenticity, and the new rules put a stop to all of this. Morrell was ready to do battle but first, in 1948, he became chief architect of Joint Promotions, which divided England up into areas which were controlled by other promoters. The idea of this was to monopolise*

*and share around the talent equally, and it worked well
for over 40 years."*

On 6 August 1945, a Boeing B-29 Super-fortress called the *Enola Gay* dropped an atomic bomb on the city of Hiroshima in Japan in an attempt to force the Japanese to surrender. The Nazis had caved in three months earlier, but the Japanese were going to fight on until the end, and something had to be done to put an end to six years of fighting. The bomb killed approximately 150,000 people outright, and nobody knew anything of radiation sickness back then so the death toll increased considerably as the years went by. Still not convinced, the Japanese fought on and a second bomb was dropped on the city of Nagasaki three days later and another 60,000 people perished and this finally brought about the end of the bloodiest war in history.

It would take many years for normality to return. In Britain most of its major cities were either destroyed or partially destroyed and there was a lot of reconstruction work to be done. Indeed, many of the wartime sanctions and restrictions would not be rescinded for a good few years and rationing did not finish until 1950. As many as 50 million people lost their lives during the war, and after the fighting ended the grieving began.

> *"For me and my family, like many others in Britain at the time, we were determined to build a new life. You wouldn't have believed it if you had surveyed the battered cities around Halifax, but people were sick and tired of death and destruction, and the desire for a peace movement like the ones we saw in the 1960s came from folks' feelings after the war. From bad usually comes good, and after all the monuments had been built and memorials attended, people dug deep and carried on because there was no other way. They hadn't gone under during the war, and they were sure as hell not giving in now. Everyone prayed for better*

times to come, and after a while new enterprises and opportunities started to spring up, and I wasn't going to be left behind so I continued to work hard and keep my ear to the ground for any kind of chance. Soon I was playing rugby league and loving every minute of it; that's when Bradford Northern became interested in me and what with the wrestling and my work in the mill, I certainly wasn't keeping all of my eggs in one basket."

Chapter Two

I Think We'll Have A Bit Of Claret Here Jack

BRITAIN WAS like a staggering alcoholic looking for one last chance to save itself from oblivion in 1946. The country was trying to make a recovery; people were starting to take steps to return to some sort of normality, but so much had been destroyed, and so many people had been killed. Millions were left homeless across Europe; the economy had collapsed, as had a lot of its industrial infrastructure, which had to be rebuilt as soon as possible. There was no money and no jobs, it was an unpleasant time to be a young lad growing up, and the freedom of the rock and roll era was still a decade away.

Instead, people waited to ignite, by listening to the music of Dorothy Squires, Frank Sinatra and Nat King Cole on the wireless. A lot of the old attitudes were starting to change though, people were screaming out against all the violence they had seen, more social freedoms were needed and many looked toward science and technology. Enough destruction had been seen, but still it was deemed necessary to conduct nuclear testing which America started at Bikini Atoll in the Pacific. They even named a little two-piece swimsuit in the area's honour, and it drove men wild when it was launched that summer. It was hoped the bikini's revealing style would cause similar reactions to those created by the nukes dropped on Japan, which is harsh marketing when you think about it.

At the end of the war Winston Churchill visited Halifax to drum up support in the run-up to the July elections in which he was defeated. "Dig For Victory" was yesterday's adventure, for the people of Britain it was time for a fresh start, but Winston did make a brief comeback in 1951 when he was re-elected at the age of 77. Massive floods hit the Calderdale area in September 1946 when the Hebble and Ryburn rivers burst their banks, as did three of the dams. Fortunately, there was no real loss of life but relief funds were set up for those who were affected. It was the Brighouse area four miles south-east of Halifax, and Walsden station to the west, rather than where the Crabtrees lived, which was hit the hardest.

Throughout the war, wrestling shows were regularly seen around the Yorkshire area. Funfairs and carnivals were affected by blackout restrictions, a lack of fuel, and no coconuts for their shy, but the shows still went on. They began to properly tour the country again once the hostilities ended, and the boxing and wrestling booths were just as popular. They were places where game young chaps could roll up their sleeves and have their arses handed to them in front of a crowd by a big square-jawed bastard with arms like tree trunks. "Last ten minutes and earn yourselves a quid" was the shout you would hear above the noise of the waltzers and the organ, and you would walk with a limp for the rest of your days.

At this point in his life Shirley was involved in rugby league as well as wrestling, and he was leaning more towards the egg-chasing as a possible escape from a life of poverty, mills and pits. He saw wrestling more as a means of fitness than anything else, although he would never have ruled anything out.

Some were lucky, and through sports, media, literature or art, they had managed to break free from what was expected of them. They say back then you could go out and leave your doors unlocked, but that was only because nobody had anything to pinch. The affluent times were approaching, and Shirley was growing up into a world where everything was changing and everybody became increasing materialistic as consumerism really bore an influence on the developed world. At 16 years old Shirley's size made him look older than his years and helped him get a summer job in Blackpool as a lifeguard, where he would be hoping to catch a glimpse of a Lana Turner lookalike in one of the new swimsuits.

The professional wrestling world was in the midst of turmoil at this point in time. The problem was discipline; people were getting hurt, and the punters had a tendency to riot if they didn't like what was going on so people were being put off. Take, for example, a wrestler called "The Vampire", who was always after blood. He would goad the crowd until they went berserk, then he would stand in the middle of the ring and tell them all to fuck off (or words to that effect), and it was usually him who ended up following his own advice when they started throwing chairs at him. It all came to a head the following year at Harringay Arena when journalists reported on a show and called it fake, and after that Norman Morrell sprang into action, and made sure Admiral Mount-Evans and his pals were alright for a drink, and got them to put the word around the manor about the new rules. Steadily, ever so steadily, order was established once again.

In January 1946, the first meeting of the United Nations was held in London as countries got together to make sure nobody could ever again do what Hitler had done, but new fears were already looming. In March, Churchill first used the words "iron curtain" in a speech in Missouri, and Ho Chi Minh was elected president of North Vietnam. You would not have recognised the significance of these events unless you had a contraption like the one in HG Wells' book *The Time Machine,* but the waters were beginning to redden once again. Even the best peace efforts couldn't put an end to the notion of war; it seemed to be the nature of the beast.

By the beginning of the 1950s, these new enemies began to reveal themselves. The main threat to Britain would come from the IRA, but the country enjoyed a relatively threat-free period until 1973, when their bombing campaign began. Another sign that things were getting back to normal was that the FA Cup Final was contested for the first time since 1939, and Derby County lifted the trophy. The year ended with the Nuremberg trials against Nazi war criminals, and the surviving instigators' right to live was withdrawn. It was at this point in his life that Shirley was faced with the biggest decision in his young life:

> *"After the war I was torn between rugby league and wrestling, and when Bradford Northern came in for me I was delighted. Although I was still training, I didn't see a future in wrestling so I went with the rugby, but I was given a bum-steer… In those days I followed our old man's philosophy. I wanted to be the hard man and I wanted to win. Of course, this wasn't a good thing on the rugby field and I was always getting sent off. After the last game I played, I was suspended for six matches and Max advised me to give up. He said I'd end up killing someone the way I was going."*

In 1947, a serious attempt to relaunch wrestling was made after the journalists had branded it "fake" and moaned about the gimmickry. With Mount-Evans in his camp Morrell put across to promoters the idea of seven separate weight divisions. Ranging from lightweight up to heavyweight, rounds would last five minutes (three for title matches), and you were given two public warnings. If you were chastised for a third time you were disqualified. Matches were usually the best of three falls, with knockouts (or count-outs) totalling an automatic two falls. The promoters liked what they saw and were in need of someone to steady the ship. They were quick to acknowledge Mount-Evans and saw it as a way to clean up a bad image. The rules pretty much echoed what was going on in America, but that was not all that changed. Using America's National Wrestling Alliance as a template, the promoters carved the business up into territories, which of course paved the way for the Joint Promotions cartel which followed in 1952.

February 1947 saw the signing of a peace treaty between the Allied nations in Paris, while in New York City the Polaroid instant camera was first demonstrated. A man named George Kidd joined Norman Morrell's gym, and he called it the hardest 18 months' training of his life. Originally from Dundee, Kidd went on to be one of the best post-war technical wrestlers, and he started fighting in the Navy. Thanks to Morrell's influence and his own hard work he ended up the lightweight champion of the world.

At the bottom of the chain, Shirley started off as an amateur, and if he had any notions of being unbeatable they were destroyed within his first couple of bouts. The youngster was taught a hard and painful lesson which he was determined to learn from. Everybody takes some kind of beating at some point in their lives, and in those early days Shirley took his fair share, but he certainly wasn't put off by it all. Instead, his interest in wrestling was growing, and he was more determined than ever to make a name for himself as it became apparent he wasn't going to make it as a professional rugby league player. Morrell was on hand and Shirley would train at his gym. With so many things to focus on he was not the quickest developer, and his professional debut was still five years away. At that point he was already watching the foods he was eating and had become well developed from all the weight-training he was doing. They say he had such an insatiable thirst for milk there was talk of buying him his own Friesian.

> "I was lucky to have many talented people around me when I was getting into it, but it wasn't all work, work, work mind you. I did my fair share of dancing and asking girls out; I had some good times before all the

crazy travelling across the country began I can tell you, and I was careful not to let anything slip to our mam. I was never a drinker, but I liked to go over to Blackpool quite a bit once I had a car. Other times, I'd stay local, go up to places like Beacon Hill where I'd sit on a wet and windy night and watch the great big clouds come rolling in across the moors, windows right down and the ice-cold rain running down my face, it was lovely. I liked my own company me, liked to see those beautiful places. Go up to what they called Bronte country, and if you were really lucky maybe you'd have a young lady in tow without her chaperone. If she trusted you, and you'd done enough wooing in the picture house (as well as buying her a Coke and a Mivvi) there might be a chance of a kiss and a bit of a cuddle, and then your mates would think you were going steady."

On 4 March 1947, future nemesis Bert Assirati became the heavyweight champion of the world when he beat Yvar Martinsen in six minutes in the last championship tournament at Haringay Arena. Born in 1908, Assirati was a cruel, hard fighter who enjoyed hurting his opponents, and he didn't like following the rules either. Some say he was one of the strongest men in the world at the time, and he was trained by Atholl Oakeley. He could also perform various weightlifting feats. He started weight-training as a 12-year-old, before becoming an acrobat, and then a wrestler, but he wasn't the friendliest of blokes and his nickname "The Islington Angel" was totally misplaced.

In the summer, the wrestling usually died away so Shirley went lifeguarding in Blackpool with future Olympic swimming coach Hamilton Smith, who described him as a pretty laid-back character. When he wasn't saving lives Shirley didn't take things too seriously, and the report logs he filled in for the people he saved were described by Smith as "mischievous" to say the least. He was certainly a presence even at that age, and Smith describes him as having an "aura" around him; people would turn their heads and look at him whenever he arrived. There was an incident a couple of years later when Shirley and Max spied a girl in trouble in the really rough seas about a hundred yards off of the Central Pier at Blackpool and Shirley swam out and saved her. On his return to the shore there was a round of applause from the crowd and a write-up in the local newspaper followed, and that was when a rumour started to circulate as a bit of a laugh. Shirley had rescued so many people, and had so many write-ups in various newspapers that people started saying Max was pushing them in off Blackpool Pier just so his brother could get them out.

> *"There's something about when you get into the sea. There's a quietness about it even though there might be a hundred people watching from shore, and you say: 'Listen, luv, relax now, because I'm going to turn you around and we're going to go back (to the shore)'… I had a stretch between North Pier and Central Pier. Holidaymakers used to run into the sea and head for the horizon and then find they didn't have the strength to head back."*

After Bradford, Shirley wasn't quite finished with rugby, and he signed for Siddal Under-18s. At the beginning of the 1947/48 season, a team photo appeared in the *Halifax Courier* which showed him as the biggest in the squad, and his blonde hair and baby face make him instantly recognisable. It was around this time that the idea of using gimmicks was really starting to take hold in Britain as wrestling started to get back on the straight and narrow. Ernie Baldwin became one of the first of the "masked men" in 1947, and he went on to be the British champion a couple of years after Peter Thornley was born. His Kendo Nagasaki character would go on to be probably the most famous man of them all to wear a mask. The Ghoul was another memorable villain starting out that year, and there was of course

Michigan-born Lou Thesz, who regained the world heavyweight championship.

On 22 May, the Cold War properly kicked off when American President Harry S. Truman signed an Act of Congress to implement the Truman Doctrine which helped Greece and Turkey in their fight against communism. Down in the south, a spaceship was reported to have crashed in Roswell, New Mexico, and alien corpses were allegedly found. There was also the joyous news that Princess Elizabeth had found her prince, and she announced her engagement to Lieutenant Philip Mountbatten five years before she was crowned Queen. As Big Daddy, Shirley would often come to the ring with the union flag draped around his shoulders, and actually meeting the Queen was one of the highlights of his career.

In the summer of 1949, the *Red Scare* was breaking news and it was certainly a worry, things were starting to get out of hand. At least the Soviet red was more pleasurable to the eye than the clinical greyness of the Nazis, but the iron curtain had come down and the space age was just around the corner. Newspapers were carrying headlines about celebrities named in FBI reports as members of the Communist Party, and stars such as Danny Kaye, Helen Keller, Dorothy Parker, and Fredric March were all in the frame. These were of course the heady days of Communist-based paranoia, and the notion of Russia spoiling for a fight wasn't exactly played down by Ivan Vlasov and his government. Suddenly, Shirley faced the real possibility of being a part of it all; if there was any fighting to be done he could well end up in the front line, and he was only too aware of this.

Conscription (or National Service as it was known in Britain) first started in 1916 to help with the war effort when the government passed the Military Services Act. It was specified that single men were liable to be called up, unless they were widowed with children, or ministers of religion. It continued until 1919, and started once again in 1939, carrying on until 1960. Expecting another sun-filled holiday season at Blackpool, Shirley was none too pleased to be missing out on it all but there was nothing he could do about it; it was his turn to do his bit for his country.

> *"I was called up on 7 June 1948, and I joined the*
> *Coldstream Guards. I had to get the train from Halifax*
> *to Catterick to fall in for the first inspection parade,*
> *and it was a rude awakening I can tell you. I'd been*
> *used to aggressive men on the rugby pitch and in the*
> *ring, but now I had a Sergeant-Major barking at me,*
> *and it was hard not to just belt him one I can tell you.*
> *It's funny because I remember that fella Robert from*
> *the 'This is Your Life' programme they did on me,*
> *coming on and telling everybody about the time we*
> *served together in the guards, and of course, I greeted*
> *him like a long-lost friend. I didn't have a ruddy clue*
> *who he was, but he obviously knew me!"*

On entering the Guards he lost his mop of blonde hair pretty much straight away as he received his first military haircut. If the truth be known it wasn't an easy time for him, and he did not fit into service life very well; he wasn't the best at being shouted at, and from day one he knew he was going to struggle even though they held wrestling matches in the afternoon, which gave him an early chance to show what he could do. His superiors were confident enough to put his name forward as a physical training instructor at the Caterham depot which allowed him to apply what he had learned in civilian life to a captive audience. In the end, his brother Max managed to get the money together to buy him out and saved him from blowing his top and ending up in a military prison. Her Majesty's Coldstream Regiment of Foot Guards are an iconic part of British culture, with their black trousers, red tunics, and Busby bearskin-hats, they are easily identifiable and this image would later be used by Shirley when he wrestled as the "Battling Guardsman".

Although National Service interrupted his wrestling career, things began to get serious for the young heel around 1949 and he turned professional a few years later. Fortunate to start off at a decent level, it was almost an honour to be hammered by some of the greats including "Roughhouse" Alf Rawlings, George Nuttall, and Jack Pye, who (like Shirley) would continue to wrestle into his 60s. None of them held back when they tackled the youngster and they did everything but mount him during those fights. If he could have grabbed a handful he would have pulled them with the force he used to get the bobbins off the machines he was that desperate. He ended many a fight covered in blood, there was no way of stopping any of them, and it was something he never forgot. The balls these men had tucked away in their shorts must have been made out of iron. It was all good experience for the youngster and he proved to the men giving him a chance that he had the guts and the will to succeed himself.

The 1950s were upon him, and deciding which path to take was the problem. His experiences in the ring certainly made him think about taking up wrestling professionally now that the rugby had fizzled out, and he had the contacts to make a go at it. Although not the most technically gifted, his strength and all-round ability, coupled with his baby face and blonde hair, made the crowd take a shine to him. Thus began his progression from a wrestler making up the numbers to a serious contender for the British title, but he had the 1950s to live through first.

At the beginning of the new decade, people were edgy about the future even though they were living in peace time. In the first few weeks of the new decade, Britain had diplomatic relations with the Republic of China withdrawn; a physicist called Klaus Fuchs admitted spying for the Soviets, and President Truman ordered the development of the hydrogen bomb in response to the Russians dropping their first one. In the end, Albert Einstein got involved and told them all to calm down, but it didn't do a lot of good as arms continued to be restocked at a frightening pace either side of the divide.

With the threat of nuclear holocaust hanging in the air people just went about their business; after all the threat was better than actual bombs falling from the sky, and conditions for the folk of Halifax steadily began to improve. Max started to train with Shirley in the town and he showed a lot of promise, and he would turn professional a few years after his older brother. As the decade progressed, jobs became easier to come by, and new housing and social facilities were built and slum housing pulled down. John Mackintosh (makers of Quality Street), and Crossley's carpets were viable alternatives if you did not fancy working in the mill or mine, and Shirley ran various jobs at this time.

Bert Assirati became the man everybody wanted to beat, but nobody wanted to fight him although he had lost the world title. He became the European wrestling champion in 1949 but left for his first tour of India the following year, and promoters and referees breathed a huge sigh of relief as they stripped him of the belt from afar. There were troubles at the end of the decade when he returned from a second Indian tour, and if they were expecting him to go quietly then they were sadly mistaken, and Shirley would witness first hand just how unhinged the man could be.

Despite the title being taken from Assirati by Joint Promotions, the British Wrestling Federation still recognised him as the champ which was a bit of a nightmare. It was only after he sustained an injury in 1960 that they mustered enough backbone to remove the title from him, but he was none too pleased about it to say the least. The authorities did not like Bert because he was a nasty bastard, and he wasn't good for the new cleaner image they were trying to promote so they wanted him out. He was a "Ripper" (meaning he liked to hurt, and be hurt) and there was no place for that in the professional ring anymore. When he wasn't fighting he was out collecting money for loan sharks, and in a fight against Jack Atherton in 1955 he whispered "I think we'll have a bit of Claret here Jack", before shattering his nose. There was absolutely no way the men in charge could allow such a character to be their champion.

It was also around this time that Shirley met a Halifax lad called Bob Sweeney, who was a couple of years younger than him and had a job in a print works. They soon struck up a great friendship, and Bob got interested in the American bodybuilding magazines which Shirley was always reading, and he became an avid follower and developed a fantastic physique himself. Shirley would wait for him outside the print works and they would go off and train and this companionship encouraged them to both work hard. Back then there were no plush gyms or health spas like today. Those kinds of swanky places with their steam rooms, weight rooms, bars, and swimming pools were the kind of places that featured in American movies only, where people like Jimmy Cagney and Humphrey Bogart lounged about in slacks and deck shoes.

If you were a weightlifter in Halifax in the late 1940s and early 1950s, you would have had a pile of weights scattered across the floor, and there would be a couple of pieces of weightlifting equipment; like benches and things if you were at one of the more established places like Norman Morrell's. If you were even luckier there might be showers and many a hard-up wrestler starting out back then saw such a luxury as a hot shower as an extra incentive to train.

Bob went on to be a successful wrestler himself; he was a very good technical fighter who was inspired by musclemen such as Spencer Churchill from Tottenham Court Road, and Bradford's Reg Park, who was Mr Universe on three occasions. He was wise enough to retire from the ring earlier than most having seen the condition of some of the older guys around him. After establishing a thriving business Bob became an expert in bodybuilding, diet, nutrition, and physiology before anybody else in the sports and fitness world started to take such things seriously, and he went on to start health clubs and modern gymnasiums before they became popular in Britain.

As the 1950s wore on there were professional debuts for wrestlers Mike Marino, Farmer John Allan, and of course a new up-and-coming star called Mick McManus who won his first welterweight title in 1949. As the years passed he would become friendly with the Crabtree brothers until they all had quite a voice in the business. After Shirley demobbed in 1952, he decided the time was right to give wrestling a go; after all there was nothing else around that he enjoyed doing. Soon he was travelling all over the place, and his brother Max followed him into the business a couple of years later, as did youngest brother Brian, and of course they had the right contacts to get themselves a leg-up in the game.

> *"Soon it was as Shirley Crabtree that I was going into action again, and promoters across Europe began to show an interest in my services but it took me a few years to get going, and I did not have an easy time of it on the way up believe me. When I think, I could have chosen a much easier career path and not experienced so much pain, but I loved wrestling, it was in my blood, and to be honest I couldn't imagine doing anything else."*

Chapter Three

Arse-Cracks And Jock Straps

BACK THEN Shirley was described as a muscular heel with a good physique and as the decade wore on he became a hit with the crowd as a "blue-eye". From the pictures of him in those early days, you can see why he used names like "The Blonde Adonis" and "Mr Universe" in the ring, and any anger issues he may have had were soon resolved. He became a solid performer who could be relied upon, and what he may have lacked in technique he certainly made up for in strength. There was a small crowd of like-minded lads going weight-training with him now, including his brother Max, Jack Wilkinson, and Bob Sweeney, who was at the time just starting to think about what he had seen in the American bodybuilding magazines, and how nice it would be to train in one of the big posh health clubs they had over there.

Bob saw it as a much healthier alternative to the sweaty old rooms they were training in, and he told Shirley this, but back then it seemed the better the gym the more dilapidated it was. Take former world middleweight champion Billy Riley's notorious Snake Pit in Wigan which was a very harsh place indeed. There were future champions who bottled out in that gym. Not only was it tough, it was a shithole, and it didn't have any of the basic amenities you would demand today. If you wanted to take a dump you grabbed a copy of yesterday's *Evening Post* and went off to find somewhere or something to take one in. Bob knew it needn't be that way; people could train in a congenial atmosphere like they were doing across the pond and avoid things like TB, lice, and black death, and maybe even take a nice hot shower, or a turn in the steam room after a workout.

It was around this time that Bob ran into Shirley's dad, and when he told his friend, he didn't really have a lot to say on the matter. Bob had never met him before, but he had heard the stories. Despite his absence, Shirley had built his father up into some sort of legendary figure, so Bob was surprised when he turned up at the print works in a van with a delivery of paper. Before he could ask him any questions, he vanished off into the ether once again without offering any explanation as to where he had been for all these years.

What effect this had on Shirley was hard to tell, but his father's rejection of him, and the rest of the family, would certainly have contributed to any anger issues he may have had as a teenager. After all, he was the only one of the three boys who really knew him; Max was just starting out in primary school when he left, and Brian never met him. The exact reasons why the old man had it away on his toes were revealed to him later, but back then, the stories Shirley told his mates about his father's influence on him, and his heroics on the pitch and in the ring, suggest he didn't lose all respect for him when he left.

Mother may have been the bulldog in the family but she cared deeply for her boys; if she had been the kind of mother to run her husband down because he had left then Shirley and Max wouldn't have held him in such high regard. She may have even known where her old man was if he was still delivering around the area, but she dealt with his absence by completely blocking him out of her thoughts, and she took any personal feelings about him with her when she died in 1970.

Shirley went on to regard the city of Newcastle with fondness and later, the Geordie crowd returned that fondness whenever he appeared there as Big Daddy. He made his professional debut at the New St. James' Hall in 1952, which was a purpose-built venue with regular boxing and wrestling contests, and it was a fight he would never forget. It was a year of upheaval in Britain, with the death of King George VI in February; a brand-new Elizabethan era was about to begin. Almost all the coal pits were closed on Tyneside, and money was hard to come by, but the locals still loved their wrestling and the hall was packed the night Shirley's professional career began as Blondie Crabtree. It was certainly a baptism of fire, and he was pretty nervous when he first stepped into the ring to face Welsh heavyweight Sandy Orford on 14 June 1952.

Advertised as a terrific heavyweight top-of-the-bill bout, the 40-year-old former Welsh rugby league international was built like a brick shithouse, and he made short work of putting the 22-year-old to the sword. The fight wasn't really a display of skilful, acrobatic wrestling, more a contest of hammer locks, Boston crabs, and bewildering holds which Shirley was primarily on the end of. He did well coming in against a man of such skill and notability losing by two falls to one, and it was all part of the education. He went on to form a great friendship with Sandy, and would end up training at his gym.

Just like it had been as an amateur, the start of Shirley's professional career was painful and it stayed like that for a good while, but it's surprising how quick you learn when you're having pain inflicted on you regularly, and he wasn't put off. Nevertheless, there were still characters knocking around from the terrible old days, instead of decent clean contests they were out to hurt and maim, and Shirley certainly wasn't having any of that.

All wrestlers had off-days when they had been on the road for far too long, or had a row with the missus before the show, and many of them have given their opponent a good clobbering in frustration and anger. Shirley was no different, but by and large he was a clean fighter that played by the rules, and that is why he got on when he started out and rose to the top so quickly. There was a lot to be said for regular wages too, and that was one thing he did miss about the guards. In the beginning of his wrestling career he was getting the odd fight here and there, but it took a lot of hard work and he had to put in the miles, before he started to become one of the recognised faces.

The Joint Promotions cartel was formed in 1952 by Dale Martin Promotions. Its inception kept all the biggest stars within their network, and rotated them so everyone got their fair share. Territories were run by promoters from that particular area, but they all came under one big umbrella. With the organisation set up and the new rules in place, older more established promoters such as Atholl Oakeley crumbled into dust, and the abolition of entertainment tax in the 1957 Budget made everything a bit easier for Joint, which had gained control of the Mount-Evans committee.

Ted Beresford had been a top-class wrestler in the 1940s, and he moved into promoting after the war. Born in Huddersfield, he quit wrestling in 1952, and teamed up with Norman Morrell to run the Yorkshire territory. The two men had a tremendous influence on Shirley and his brothers; they trusted the boys and knew they were an honest and reliable bunch, and that they would do their best to put on a good show. The way they went about their affairs was a big influence on Max in particular; he had an interest in business as well as fighting, and he learned a lot from them. Although he could never match his older brother in size and power he was the most technically gifted of the three, and he would go on to be crowned lightweight wrestler of the year in 1961.

With Morrell and Beresford running Yorkshire, Dale & Martin running London, Billy Best responsible for Liverpool, George de Relwyskow Scotland, and others running the rest of the territories, Joint had the wrestling in the bag, and this left very little room for wrestlers to negotiate. By keeping the wages low they could survive and grow as a firm, and rotating the talent meant nobody else could get in on the act.

"I fought them all in those early years. Back then, the wrestling season ran from September to May, and after that, all the heavyweights went off to Europe for the summer and I went down to Blackpool lifeguarding for the first few years. I think it was probably my upbringing which made me such a tough character; I was very determined and after a while I was just about making a wage. Nobody ever went into wrestling to become a millionaire like you can nowadays in America with the WWF, but they were very good days. Full of hard men like Bill Joyce, Jack Pye from Doncaster, Dai Sullivan from Tonypandy, and Killer Ken Davies, you got to know them all. We were on the road for most of the week and you had to try to get on else life became unbearable. We were all in it together, and you've got to remember there weren't any motorways in the early 1950s; it was all back-roads and we spent many hours cooped up in the back of a van or a car. It wasn't easy if the bloke you were sat next to for 300 miles had smelly feet, or had been on the real ale and pickled eggs the night before, but you had to get on. If not, you'd sort it out in the car park which the bosses didn't like. They'd rather you had a row with the bloke who refused to pay you back, in the ring."

The early 1950s saw debuts for fighters such as Mike Marino, Orig Williams, and Judo Al Hayes who had won the British heavyweight title at Harringay Stadium the year before Joint was formed. Another man who would come to the fore in the Crabtrees' life was Norman F. Berry, who started out working in the office for Norman Morrell running all the shows. The fact that he was from Halifax gave him something in common with the Crabtrees, and he would become the "authority figure" the boys needed to get a foothold in the business themselves when the time came.

By now, a lot of wrestlers were getting annoyed with the Joint stranglehold. Rebellion was in the wind and when Berry fell out with Morrell the seeds were sown. He decided to go his own way and was looking for people he could trust to come in on the venture. It was a case of the Crabtree boys being the right people, in the right place, at the right time, and with another chap called Jack Taylor they set up Twentieth-Century Wrestling in 1958.

There were others trying to get in on the act too, the Leicester-based Alliance of Independent Promoters also starting up at this time, as did Paul Lincoln Promotions. Born in Australia, Lincoln was another big piece to the Crabtree jigsaw, and he would have a huge influence on the brothers as they took their first tentative steps in business. Lincoln also enjoyed a spot of wrestling himself, and he became pretty good in a mask and black tights as Doctor Death. Originally arriving in Britain in the early 1950s, he had worked as a bodyguard for a currency dealer before becoming the co-owner of 2i's coffee bar in Soho, London. In those rooms, above the smell of tobacco and coffee beans, rock and roll was first launched in Britain, and acts such as Tommy Steele, and Cliff Richard and The Shadows came to prominence. After gaining a contract to promote his wrestling business through Granada cinemas in 1959, Lincoln was suddenly a very popular man and is considered by many to be one of the greatest promoters of all time.

Picture if you will, a blonde-haired, blue-eyed, muscular Yorkshireman approaching that point in the 1950s when it all suddenly went boom. Did he have the quiff, the white t-shirt, and black biking leathers like James Dean? The answer is no; Shirley was a down-to-earth chap who spent most of his life in a tracksuit even when he wasn't working, but it would be wrong to say he didn't get among it when all of those hormones were bubbling away inside of him.

Towards the mid-point of the 1950s, things in Britain started to improve dramatically, suddenly it all started to feel a bit easier and jobs were not so hard to find. In 1954, American Bill Haley and his band the Comets, as well as Elvis Presley, recorded the first real rock and roll songs, although both failed to reach the national Billboard charts on initial release. It was when Haley's song 'Rock Around The Clock' featured in the teen rebellion film *Blackboard Jungle* that the whole rock and roll movement really kicked off, and paved the way for people like Little Richard, Jerry Lee Lewis, Chuck Berry, and Carl Perkins.

American troops stationed in Britain passed on this music, and told stories about the Teddy Boys, and Britain gradually caught on to the craze. In early 1955, *Variety* magazine claimed "rock and roll will be gone by June" but it obviously misjudged the mood. Figures such as James Dean, Johnny Cash, and Buddy Holly all helped to shape and expand the movement, and by 1956, American records were starting to top the UK charts. Soon, British artists were getting in on the act, but it wasn't until 1958 that Cliff Richard and The Shadows became the first "authentic" British rock and roll band when their song 'Move It' reached number two.

> *"Oh yes, I was a big fan of Cliff definitely; I used to love rock n roll music back in the day; I still do. In fact, talking about it all reminds me of a story from when we first started out and were at home celebrating one of our first breaks. For some reason, somebody had chained an old bike to the wall outside and it had been there for months rusting away. As I recall, we were all stood in our mam's front room celebrating when we heard someone knocking on the door. I opened it, and this fella was stood there, and he asked me if anyone was doing anything with the bike because he wanted to use it to go see Elvis Presley, so I told him to help himself. He was as nutty as a fruitcake and I didn't have the heart to tell him Elvis lived in America."*

The dance halls of Halifax were erupting to this crazy new sound and Shirley (now sporting big sideburns) and his brothers were

51

thinking there may be a few quid to be made from it all seeing as they were the sober ones. To gain a bit of extra money Shirley and Max had started to work the door of various local nightclubs, and the difference in their size was comical. Shirley was over 6ft 2in and a heavyweight wrestler, while his lightweight brother was a lot smaller. They looked smart in their suits, and they weren't overly aggressive like some. Indeed, Shirley was rather laid-back for a bouncer, but if you were to get on the wrong side of him you may well have been eating your breakfast the next morning through a straw in a hospital ward. He worked a few different doors, including Cats Whiskers in Halifax, and the Majestic Ballroom in Leeds, and they worked the doors to some of the places run by Jimmy Savile.

When they weren't working, Shirley and his fellow body-builders would take the trek out into the sticks and visit Sandy Orford on his farm near Bradford some mornings to train. Sandy had finished playing professional rugby league in 1947, but a good part of his career had been disrupted by the war. A hard but decent second row during the era of contested scrums, it was just as bad coming up against him on the pitch as it was in the ring. Sandy was a respectable bloke who had the honour of not only beating all three of the Crabtree brothers in the ring, but their father too. If you found yourself up against him in any contact sport you knew it was going to be painful, and the sharp learning curve usually embedded itself into some fleshy part of your head or body. Despite the war, Sandy still managed a handful of caps for his beloved Wales before turning to professional wrestling.

Parking up the car and avoiding the cow pats, Shirley and the lads would make their way through the farmyard and into the barn where Sandy would either be training, or teaching in a ring he had set up in the middle. It would not be unheard of for a chicken or a hen to flap into the barn, and sometimes even the ring, and many of those who were plucky enough to invade ended up in the pot come Sunday. You can imagine the communication problems between the Yorkshire lads, and Sandy with his Pontypool twang.

In later years as Big Daddy, Shirley had to talk to all sorts of dignitaries and plummy television people. Known for reciting passages by people such as John Keats and Oscar Wilde, he hated his accent, and he tried to talk in a "posh" voice to sound less like a Yorkshireman when interviewed, which made members of his family roll about with laughter.

Atholl Oakeley's last throw of the dice came in 1952, when he brought in a man billed at 8ft 4in and 50 stone who fought under the name of Gargantua. Real name Kurt Zehe, he was a big unit to say the least, and he was Germany's first heavyweight. He was brought to the country in an attempt to revive the "all-in" style but the problem was finding somebody to fight him, although he was paired with fighters like Ed Bright, Primo Carnera, and Bert Assirati.

What could you do to a monster like that without a weapon? A big deal at the time was when he fought Jack Doyle in a bout Oakeley hoped would re-establish him as the UK's top promoter. Unfortunately, the contest was terrible, there wasn't much to see, and this spelt the end for Oakeley, and for big men fighting, until the super-heavyweight division became popular in the 1970s, and was of course dominated by Daddy and Haystacks.

In the mid-1950s, Shirley was first offered the chance to wrestle abroad, which until then had meant a fight on the Isle of Wight. He had never been abroad as a civilian, and he was looking forward to seeing countries such as Belgium, Germany, and France. Later, he was given the chance to go to Vienna which was a city he absolutely adored. He would return there many times in years to come to either fight or take a holiday with his family, and he would have definitely enjoyed having a holiday home in Austria because of the icy climate. The nearest he ever got to owning property abroad was when he was offered the chance to buy an apartment in Monte Carlo next to Rock Hudson's pad for not a lot of money at all. Although he turned the offer down he did wonder in later years, when prices rocketed, how much it would have been worth.

"I was never one to be flash; in fact, I didn't do money at all. When I got famous as Big Daddy and we started to make a few quid, my wife Eunice handled all of that. As long as I had clean kit, a bit of snack in my bag, and a fiver in my trouser pocket I was happy. We didn't like to stop over whenever we were away fighting like some folk did, we always tried to get back to Halifax that same night which could be a killer, especially if you'd been wrestling in somewhere like Cornwall."

When Harringay Arena closed in 1954, Atholl Oakeley's venture had come to an end, which meant Joint Promotions were the only major players left in the game at the time. With an old-style champion in Bert Assirati, he did them a favour when he quit and went to work for Paul Lincoln, and he took the British championship belt (re-claimed from Ernie Baldwin after he returned from a tour of India) with him. By the beginning of the 1960s, there really was no place for Bert as the Mount-Evans style dominated, and he finally retired in 1963 aged 52.

Spencer Churchill was another notable fighter around at the time, but he is mentioned here because he was a bodybuilder and wrestler admired by Bob Sweeney and the Crabtree brothers. He had a magnificent physique, beaten only by Bradford's Reg Park in Sweeney's reckoning, who claimed the Mr Universe title three times between 1951 and 1965. Churchill won the light-heavyweight version of *Britain's Most Developed Man* in 1954, and then turned to pro wrestling. Never top of the bill, he was good to watch, and was given the nickname Mr Muscles Unlimited, and is still training at the time of writing.

Early fights of notability for Shirley were against Franz Vorhemus in October 1954, Dai Sullivan in November, and Bert Royal, Les Kellett, and Masambula the African witch-doctor were on the same bill. He also fought Rex Harrison at the Baths Hall in Keighley on Wednesday 15 December 1954, before he was let go by Joint Promotions. It was then that he first looked at using a gimmick in the ring.

His appearances in those formative years as a pro had been infrequent and sometimes below par. He had been angered by some of the more established wrestlers who would try to hurt up-and-coming fighters like him because they didn't want their livelihoods challenged, and of course, he gave it back to them. The clean-up that took place within wrestling happened before the television people gave Joint the contract, and by then Shirley was still out in the wilderness with them, his TV debut still a good few years away.

Appearing as both Ex-Guardsman Wilkinson and Gunboat Smith to name just two, he would revert back to his real name once he returned to Joint in the 1970s. With the backing of some pretty prominent figures, it all started to slowly come together for Shirley after that, and then suddenly there was a new British champion for the TV generation. Bill Joyce was among the first to make use of the exposure; he won the title in 1955 and held on to it for most of the next 12 years.

Chapter Four

A Dump In Glasgow For The King

O N 1 November 1955, the Vietnam War started between the South Vietnamese Army, who were supported by the United States, and the Communist North, who were allied with the Viet Cong. America got involved because they did not want to see a communist takeover so in the very beginning they backed French fighting forces before sending in their own troops.

Britain meanwhile, was in the grip of fish-finger mania a couple of years before the cod wars began. Clarence Birdseye's tasty frozen breadcrumb sticks went on sale for the very first time, although Captain Birdseye (the white-bearded old sailor who munched the things like there was no tomorrow) did not appear on TV screens for another generation. It is surprising nobody challenged Clarence's concept; instead his frozen sticks became a regular part of the school, and evening meal, as tabard-wearing mums and dinner ladies went mad for them. They were defrosted and cooked of course, and it is safe to say they were a big hit despite the obvious flaw. It is true that some of the more pulpous creatures you may find in the sea have tentacles and appendages, at least the ones you can cave in with the edge of a shovel do, but never has a fish been caught with fingers.

It was the same crazed mothers, fathers, grans, granddads, and their cod-and-breadcrumb-pumped kids, who sat down and watched the first televised wrestling show, which aired on 9 November, 1955, with Mike Marino v Francis St Clair as the main event, and it had been filmed several days before. Soon, the shows were a regular occurrence, and people got sucked into the storylines as the drama unfolded. It was usually a case of one wrestler looking for revenge over another, and many who saw those first shows on their TVs went to watch the live ones, which were on in most towns and cities at least once a month.

There was always the good guy, and the bad guy, and these characters sent the crowd alternating between states of excitement and despair. Old ladies across the land would swear at their TV sets, and then go to the shows hell-bent on revenge. Excited at the sight of fighters such as Bert Royal, Jackie Pallo, and Mick McManus with his hairy chest, they usually sat in ringside seats, or next to the gangway, and jabbed at the bad guys with their knitting needles and umbrellas as they made their entrance. Not quite considered a terrorist group, gung-ho senior citizens were to be feared, and there is many a wrestler out there who sustained an injury from a normally sweet, innocent old lady who was secretly a sadist.

With November being so late in the year (which wasn't uncommon), it was pretty cold, and the drop in temperature usually thinned out the numbers a bit. Somehow, some of the meanest, gnarled old crones hung on to life during those frozen months, and managed to return to the wrestling year after year. You could almost see their knitting needles gleaming in the half-light of the West Ham Baths that first night in front of the TV cameras; they certainly added a tinge of brightness to the audience if you were at home watching in bleak black and white.

Riding high in the music charts at the time was a song called 'Cry Me A River' by Julie London, and this song described West Ham Baths down to a tee that first night. Only the voice of commentator Kent Walton, greeting grappling fans with his mid-Atlantic drawl, lifted the spirits. It wasn't what you would have called high-octane. However, wrestlers now had the chance to become household names, and there were titles out there to be won, some more legitimate than others.

For the first time in history, becoming a champion meant you were instantly a television personality, and for some that was everything. It superseded the poor wages they were paid. There was money to be made but most of it stopped with the promoters, and it was all made possible thanks to the ending of the BBC's 18-year television monopoly in 1955. ABC and ATV were two of the first ITV franchises, and when they began showing wrestling people went mad for it. It was Joint Promotions that had the exclusive TV contract, and the best fight of the night (Ray Hunter versus Tony Mancelli) wasn't even televised.

There was quite a bit to celebrate in the grappling world in 1955. Not only had it cleaned up its act, it was on its way to becoming a regular part of TV scheduling. With the wrestling on the box, and the new Airfix collection of scale models going on sale for the first time, people lived the high life that Christmas. Short trousers, Pedigree dolls and woollen tank-tops were still all the rage. Commitment was just around the corner for Shirley who was now 25 years old; he had been going steady with a local girl called Marilyn Kelly for quite some time, and she was the sister of Brian's friend Phillip. They wed in Halifax in the summer of 1956, and lived happily in Bell Hall, near Saville Park, for a while, until the rowing started and the marriage descended into chaos. Marilyn was described by Brian Crabtree as "an absolute super-bitch" and they were eventually divorced. From then on it was a case of "once bitten twice shy" for Shirley, who was in no rush to be going steady again anytime soon. What's more, the brothers' business relationship with Paul Lincoln was developing quite nicely, and Shirley started wrestling for him and other independent promoters around that time.

As the 1950s moved towards the final couple of years, more and more British rock and roll bands were springing up to challenge their American counterparts. Another US import was world heavyweight champion Lou Thesz, who came to Britain to wrestle in 1957, and in that same year Mike Marino became light-heavyweight world champ for the first time. In America, Elvis Presley appeared on the *Ed Sullivan Show*, but they would only film him from above the waist because of the effect his gyrating hips had on teenage girls, who would have gone into meltdown at the sight of a wrestler in a leotard with half a lob.

And of course the religious nuts loved all of the controversy. It gave them their 15 minutes of fame, and some of them were dangerous too. They were the same "holier than thou" people causing trouble for Doctor Martin Luther King down south. Britain had her own version of the troubles with organisations like the National Front, and trouble ignited when West Indian and South Asian settlers started to come into the country around this time.

Much to the dismay of the USA, the space-race began on Friday 4 October 1957 without them. The Russians launched into orbit the first artificial satellite Sputnik 1, and the news was accompanied by a strange telemetric beeping from space, which was on all of the wires. It was a major talking point that night at the dance at the Victoria Hall in Halifax, which was the place to go if you wanted to bop to all the latest hits (at least on Wednesdays and Fridays). There was no chance of getting tanked up though; they only served soft drinks and milkshakes, although the Teddy Boys would be there with their concealed hip flasks, and hardly a hair out of place. If anyone was caught with drink by Shirley and Max who were working the door, there would be no more dancing with the pretty girls with their sticky-out petticoats, pig-tails, and bob shoes. They might even get a slap or a closer look at the pavement if they were full of lip, but there wasn't usually much trouble.

By January 1957 Shirley had won his first 15 fights at Joint, and in an interview he revealed his ambition to be the heavyweight champion of the world. Outside the ring the brothers had decided the time was right to take the plunge into the business world, and they first started to put their local knowledge of the nightclub scene to good use by organising dances in the Labour Rooms on St James Road in Halifax.

There were a few places around to hear good music back then, but they went on to run Halifax's most trendy nightclub in the 1960s, and they brought in some of the best acts in the hit parade to perform live.

Being so far away from London, the town was usually way behind in terms of what was happening in the world of fashion, music, and what the word was on the street, but that all changed once the Beatles and the Merseybeat sound became the most happening scene in the world in the early 1960s, and the brothers were able to capitalise. Only 57 miles from mop-top Liverpool, Halifax was still a saveloy and chip butty kind of a town, and John Lennon and his band never did play in the Calderdale area. When Beatlemania hit, America's rock and roll dominance ended. Buddy Holly was dead, Jerry Lee had married his 13-year-old cousin, Little Richard had found God, and Chuck Berry could go play with his ding-a-ling someplace else. The Fab Four were taking over.

Elvis did pop into Britain in 1960, if only a brief stop-over at Glasgow Prestwick Airport, but not once did his blue suede shoes hit the streets of the city. He also met the Beatles in August 1965, but the earth didn't move for any of them then either. The result of all of this messing about was the fact that suddenly, Halifax was not so out on a limb anymore and, after holding the dances at the Labour Rooms, the Crabtrees were able to think bigger.

The next thing they did was put an advert in the *Daily Courier* on 11 December 1959, advertising the fact that the Marlborough Hall was up for hire. After that, they started to organise dances there themselves. The place was a dump, but they gave it a bit of a spruce up, a lick of paint, and called it "Big Daddies" as they jumped right on the whole Bert Ives stereotype, and suddenly all the cool cats were hanging out.

It was around this time that Max turned to pro wrestling himself and Shirley was now established as a top heel for a variety of independent promoters. Max fought Count Bartelli around this time in Hanley. Bartelli was masked, and he was beaten using a grapevine and should really have been de-masked in defeat. Max's progress was faster than Shirley's and the late 1950s and early 1960s were a very happy time for the brothers, and it wasn't just Shirley fighting all the big names. Max followed his brother by fighting some great wrestlers during that period, including Black Butcher Johnson, Quasimodo, Leo Demeteral, and Paul Lincoln himself as Doctor Death. With the amount of sleep Shirley was getting back then it is surprising that he managed to wrestle at all:

> *"In those early days, I was always working. I was life-guarding during the day and working the doors in the evening, and then we were running dances and venues ourselves. Brian was a builder, and whilst he was off up the road building Illingworth Fire Station, I was working as Max's labourer for Halifax council. One day we were inside this house, and Max was building a stone fireplace, I had been working most of the night, and I'd only had a couple of hours' kip, so I lay down on the sofa in my big work boots and had a bit of a sleep, while he carried on. A council inspector came to check up on our work, and Max was shitting himself because he could hear me snoring away. He insisted on coming in to examine Max's work, and he saw me asleep, but we managed to get away with it because we convinced him it was my house."*

If Shirley had wanted a sleep, he would have had one no matter what any council inspector said. He wouldn't have been overly bothered if he had got the sack, although he was never keen on letting his brother down. It was easy enough to walk into another job, and he was quite well known around Halifax, so he wouldn't have been out of work for long. He wasn't good at being told what to do, and this is why he'd had problems in the Coldstream Guards.

The money in wrestling was terrible, and he needed to be doing all of these other bits and pieces just to make ends meet. He was starting to become popular across the United Kingdom, and was also known in Europe, although he could have probably earned more brass doing factory work than wrestling. He felt this was unfair, and he was not the first wrestler to have a slanging match with the British Wrestling Federation over low wages. There were no expenses or chauffeur-driven limousines back then, you could be the champion of the whole of Great Britain, and if your car had broken down, and you couldn't get a lift they wouldn't worry. Just as long as you turned up with your belt and your leotard to defend your title, you could get the bus for all they cared.

These were the days of proper hard men wrestling, way before spray-tans and anabolic steroids. Nobody gave a damn about health and safety, and the inception of BUPA was years away, which is why most of the older wrestlers still around today are in such a state. Many have dodgy knees, ankles, hips, or walk with a stoop. If you went over the ropes and landed on a table, a chair, or the floor, it bloody well hurt no matter whether you had learned to fall or not.

With their fingers in a few pies there was a feeling that the Crabtree lads were up-and-coming, and maybe there was a little bit of resentment from one or two others who weren't perhaps as in with the "in-crowd" as they were. To be fair, there was a streak of arrogance running through all three brothers at times, but this would not have been uncommon in anyone as young as they were, and in the position they were in.

Take Shirley for example. In the early 1960s he was a champion wrestler, and a nightclub owner and he had only just entered his 30s. He was not the worst of the three. Brian has been described by many as suffering from "ego problems", and Max treated more than one person like something he had scraped from the bottom of his shoe.

Out of the three, Shirley was the most down-to-earth, but catch him on a bad day and he could be a nightmare. There were many occasions after the fight when he had sat down beside the ring and signed hundreds of autographs, or visited sick kids in the hospital in his spare time. There was also an occasion when he wouldn't come out and sign and he left a crowd of disappointed kids all waiting for him outside.

Being on the road so much and having to get back home to Halifax every night must have been hell, but people only want to focus on the negative side of things and reinforce the story that child favourite Big Daddy did not like kids at all. I dare say there were times when he was sick to death of kids and parents, but as Big Daddy, Shirley spent many hours of his personal time doing things for charity and it is unfair to knock him for that.

Many wrestlers could only dream of gaining the fame Shirley achieved, and they were streets ahead of him in the big-headed stakes. And while we are straightening things out, let's look at another misconception about Max being the brains of the bunch. It was Shirley who was more than likely to come up with a realistic idea that would actually work. Max was good at business; he created some fantastic wrestling characters, but it was Shirley who pulled him back down to earth when he was away with the fairies. By the early 1960s they had already taken several steps up the ladder in both the fight game, and in the business side of things, although Brian's short wrestling career came to an end in 1962 when he broke his leg and his doctor advised him to quit.

Shirley was an intensely private man who didn't like a lot of fuss, even more so when he was at the height of his fame. Deep down, he was gutted about his marriage breaking up as any decent man would be, and when he was sat there in the small hours working it all through in his head he would have drawn parallels with his dad, although Shirley never thought the grass was greener anywhere else. He may have sometimes been pissed off with situations, but most of the time he was happy with his lot, perhaps until the limelight started to fade in the late 1980s, and he should have retired and had more time for himself.

The women he chose to have in his life were always very strong and independent, and it is a shame he never managed to find a truly harmonious bond, although of course there were many good memories for him to look back upon when he reached his twilight years.

The brotherly bond between Shirley and Max was put under stress when the business was coming to an end and they were advancing in years, but in the beginning all three of them stuck together like brothers should. When their father left the family huddle, Shirley and his brothers grew bigger shoulders to keep it all together for themselves and their mother, and it was this kind of relationship which later held the whole of their wrestling empire together. Shirley would become the main attraction; Brian a referee and MC, and Max was the boss. Many of the wrestlers who worked for him felt hard-done-to by his methods, but managing a bunch of wrestlers (many with ego problems themselves) was never going to be easy. Some felt they weren't looked after, but it had always been that way, and Shirley had no control over any of these things. Did it all go to the Crabtree brothers' heads? Of course it did at times, but the wagon rolled on for another two decades once they gained control, when the wheels could just as easily have come off.

The character "Big Daddy" first came to the public's imagination in the 1958 film *Cat On A Hot Tin Roof*, and was (as we have already mentioned) played by actor Bert Ives, and Shirley's third wife Eunice was fond of the film.

In February that year, an aeroplane carrying the Manchester United football team crashed and 23 people were killed. They were on their way home from a European Cup game against Red Star Belgrade, and they had stopped in Munich, Germany, to refuel. They were trying to take off in freezing cold weather when the tragedy happened. Among the dead were eight players from the "Busby Babes" side, and Sir Matt Busby himself was administered the last rites before making a dramatic recovery.

In April, it all started kicking off in Cuba as Fidel Castro's revolutionary army began their attack on Havana, and the cod wars finally started between Britain and Iceland regarding fishing rights in the North Atlantic. The first number one record in Britain that year was 'Great Balls Of Fire' by Jerry Lee Lewis, which would have made an excellent bit of entrance music if you had been a little over ambitious with the Deep Heat and not washed your hands.

It was during 1958 that Shirley cut all ties with Joint and joined Max who was involved in starting Twentieth-Century promotions that year. Their slice of the pie was little more than a couple of flakes of hard pastry off the top of a very juicy dish with Joint enjoying the lion's share. Times were tough for the independent promoters, but there was a bit of hope when Bert Assirati split away from Joint as reigning champion, and they of course considered the belt vacant. The BWF still recognised Bert as the champ, so it didn't work out too badly for him, and before he knew it Paul Lincoln was knocking on his caravan door with a contract, and the backing of a consortium of independent promoters all hanging about in the awning. They started up a rival championship with George Kidd and Ken Joyce which they build around Bert, who was absolutely delighted seeing as he was getting on a bit.

Without the TV, the independents were way behind before they got the deal with Granada Cinemas. While all of this was happening Joint held a tournament for the vacant belt which Billy Joyce won. It was then that it all got a little bit confusing. With two champions the politics kicked in, but it was all about money rather than wrestling. As the year moved on, Bobby Barnes made his debut for Dale and Martins (Joint's representatives in London) and fought Mick McManus, Jackie Pallo, and Len Wilding within the first few weeks. A very colourful wrestler, he was like John Inman's character Mr Humphries in sequin-covered drawers, and he strutted around the ring like a peacock with his long blonde locks. Of course owning ladies' hairdressers meant he was never far away from a good shampoo and set, and when he wasn't doing that he was teaming up with Adrian Street to form the Hells Angels tag team and beating people around the ring.

Working during the day, and then at night in the clubs and dance halls until the small hours, would have taken its toll on the Crabtree brothers. Add to that all the miles they travelled in all kinds of weather, which was what you had to do if you wanted to get established and maybe have a crack at one of the titles. And of course, when you go to Aberdeen, Alloa, Penzance, and Dover you still had to have enough left in you to put on a good show. It was almost a thankless job, save the applause from the crowd if you weren't a villain, and Shirley's life became totally dominated by the job like many other wrestlers working the circuit.

Over the years, he missed out on a hell of a lot of stuff going on at home. It could be a harsh way to live especially if you were stuck in a town because of snow or ice, or you were so tired you were seeing two sets of white lines and dancing penguins in the middle of the road. There were even times when Shirley spent the night in the car with the engine running just so he didn't freeze to death.

February 1959 was a pretty harsh month all round. On the third, Buddy Holly, The Big Bopper, and Ritchie Valens were killed in yet another aeroplane crash, but this one happened in Clear Lake, Iowa, USA.

The 1950s ended pretty quietly for Shirley all things considered, and at that time his marriage was almost at breaking point. Emile Ford and the Checkmates ended the decade at number one in the hit parade with their record 'What Do You Want To Make Those Eyes At Me For?' and there was more trouble brewing. A new British heavyweight champion was needed, and Shirley would be offered the biggest chance of his eight-year-old professional career.

Chapter Five

Swinging Sixties

AND SO, the 1960s began. The decade which would change mankind's attitudes and lifestyles more than any other in recorded history was about to get underway. From small seeds, the leaves and branches of opportunity, peace and love, spread outwards and tried to embrace the world. An anti-war feeling was in the air; the first half of the 20th century had been unique in the fact that its conflicts had killed more people en masse than any other period in history. The methods of destruction, and the levels of violence human beings had stooped to in search of power, and the chance to redefine borders, were shocking. The line which showed where one country ended and another began could have been marked out with a thick white line made from the powdered bones of the millions of people who fought and died, and it could have run right the way across Europe. People were sick of death and destruction, and the 1960s would see a complete role reversal as established attitudes and institutions were challenged. The peace movement was about to begin, and the pilgrimage to Woodstock would take place in 1969.

The decade began with a fresh new face; Senator John F. Kennedy announced his candidacy for the Democratic presidential election which he won, but this sealed his fate and he was shot dead in Dallas, Texas, three years later. Around the same time as Kennedy's announcement, British Prime Minister Harold

Macmillan was doing what MPs are best at, talking through their posteriors. He delivered his famous "winds of change" speech to a South African Parliament high on boerewors, baked beans, Maheu, and apartheid; they would have gone through a lot of toilet paper consuming all of that, and keeping such company. Indeed, flatulence was very close to the rhetoric Supermac was applying to an already rolling stone.

Back home, Shirley was receiving news of an injury to Bert Assirati, and the BWF stripped him of the British heavyweight title while he was recovering, rather than sending him a get well card and a bunch of flowers. With Bert being on such bad terms with many of the promoters they wanted rid, and now that Shirley was back in the fold he was given a shot at the British championship, and he defeated the "Mighty Strangler" Ed Bright in a match set up in Leicester on 4 October to contest the vacant belt. The legitimacy of this title has come into question in the past as there were a lot of different titles around at the time, and the one he won wasn't considered a proper Mount-Evans contest. The truth is, Shirley was a worthy champion. If anything it was a tougher belt to win; Assirati did not play nicely when he was defending it, and many of the wrestlers who fought Bert for the belt had to battle for their lives. After winning the championship Shirley was contacted by Belgian wrestling promoter Leon Pascal, and that is how he got a shot at the European title.

With 28-inch thighs, a chest of 55 inches, and 19-inch upper biceps, he was a lean 19-stone fighter who did not prescribe to the old style of wrestling so he certainly added an element of legitimacy to the title. Like Assirati, he was a hardman; unlike him, he was fair, and he used his power to develop effective moves such as the headlock, and he added the European title the following year when he defeated 28-stone Felix Miquet at the Palais de Sports in Brussels in front of a packed house of 20,000.

In one of the most vicious matches seen in a long time Miquet really gave it to his opponent as he defended a title he had held for ten years. In the end a crotch hold and body press was the combination that won it for Shirley but he was not without injury. As he hobbled out through the ropes streaming with blood, he was in absolute agony having dislocated a disc in his back, and torn a cartilage. Yet none of this mattered at that precise moment as he stood beneath the lights enjoying the feeling. It was a defining moment for Shirley; how far he had come since those early days at Normal Morrell's gym when the lightweight champion Bernard Murray had first taken him on the mats and taught him how to wrestle.

On winning the title, Shirley was noted in one magazine article as a man of immense strength who was often likened to Georg Hackenschmidt. He had a clean style, and a fine sense of fair play who relied on more solid textbook wrestling than the acrobatics of the modern-day wrestler. Bert Assirati was about to try to give Shirley a bit of stick; he stood up and heckled him at at least one of his fights, and it was all totally unstaged by any of the promoters. Folklore has it that he harassed Shirley out of the game, but there is no evidence to substantiate any of these claims.

Shirley wasn't scared of Bert, and people in the know such as Bob Sweeney, Mick McManus, and Brian Dixon could not add weight to these claims when asked, and they have been backed up by wrestling historians and writers Robert Cope and Russell Plummer. Shirley carried on wrestling regularly, although he quietened things down in around 1966, and fought mainly around the Blackpool area until his comeback in the early 1970s for Joint. Add to this the fact that Assirati had been beaten by Ed Bright (which pretty much finished off his career), and then Shirley scored a victory over Ed in a contest to find a new champion, there really was no need for him to go and get maimed by the 52-year-old. What Bert should have done was play by the rules; he'd had a good run, and fought all over the world. His feats of strength were well known, but his type of wrestling was a dying trade, and it was time for a new generation to have a chance.

Max had done great things promoting independently, and later getting the brothers back on board was a good move by the bosses at Joint Promotions. Indeed, Twentieth-Century received praise for their form of promotion which was described as ahead of its time, despite the fact they were only running shows on a part-time basis. Likened to a small subsidiary in America, and with Norman F. Berry overseeing the financial aspects, they managed to grab a big enough slice of the pie to make the bosses at Joint sit up and take notice.

From an early age, Max believed Shirley was something special; he was the kind of person who stood out in a crowd, and he was over-protective of his brother. He knew he was going places, and it was a case of protecting both their interests, as well as their younger brother Brian. Barnsley wrestler Sam Betts, who started out at a gym owned by Charlie Glover, the father of wrestler and actor Brian Glover, recalls Max telling him that there would be no more work if he hurt Shirley, but Sam wasn't a particularly dirty fighter. He certainly didn't entertain any of the old methods; wrestlers were not in it to have limbs broken. If they didn't work they didn't get paid, it was as simple as that, and many of them had mouths to feed. There was always going to be a bit of resentment because of the way Max singled out his brother, and this became more apparent once Shirley was using the Big Daddy gimmick. There were other fighters around who did not receive the limelight they should have done because of the Daddy bandwagon, but that was the nature of the game. Whoever was selling most seats was the one receiving most of the attention.

JFK wasn't the only big news at the beginning of the 1960s. Back home in the Halifax area the headline story had nothing to do with politics, but it still caused a flap. Old Harry Taylor was left gutted when his poultry farm in the village of Mytholmroyd went up in flames one night and choked his 5,000 chickens. March was a busy month too. Not only did Denis Law sign for Manchester City from Huddersfield Town for a national record fee of £55,000; Elvis Presley left the US Army after serving two years of National Service. Civvy Street wasn't so kind on the King and his music career this time around. He would find it harder to score hit records during the early 1960s, with new rock and roll acts such as the Beatles, the Rolling Stones, Bob Dylan, and Simon and Garfunkel dominating the charts. He did manage a massive comeback towards the end of the decade, and into the 1970s, but "The Pelvis" had gone. Replaced by bingo wings and a massive stomach, the King had more chins than a Chinese phonebook, and he chomped so many cheeseburgers it made his colon expand. He was found dead in his bathroom on 16 August 1977, and while his death was not treated as suspicious, he had high levels of painkiller, sleeping pills, and burger relish in his blood.

At the beginning of the1960s, there was further movement throughout the wrestling world too. Not only were the costumes and leotards getting ever more leery, but the new British champion Shirley Crabtree was starting to get some media exposure in magazines and newspapers, and he fought the US fighter The Monster at Granby Halls in Leicester in a return heavyweight challenge. People were told to turn up sharpish for the "tremendous duel", and the fight was billed as: "An international scoop at terrific expense." It was nothing like the publicity Shirley would receive as Big Daddy, but it was enough to establish his reputation in a very tough trade where grapplers came and went in the blink of an eye. One night after he had finished wrestling he was given the shock of his life when a figure from his past suddenly turned up out of the blue:

> *"He stayed away a long time [Shirley's father], but when I was about 30, I was wrestling one night in Cleethorpes and he was in the audience. He came up after and said: 'It's been a long time, and before anything happens to me, let's make it up.' So we did... His differences were all with my mother – he'd been a marvellous father. He'd had dumbbells made for me and my two brothers, had a little mat in front of the fire, and taught us to hand-balance and wrestle... When he went, my brothers and I made a little gym of*

> *our own, excluding him. We made a mat from straw and canvas and had broom handles with flat irons on them. We were really dedicated. The roots he put there stayed with us all our lives."*

Despite all the rhetoric the relationship with his father was not maintained, but this would not be the last he, or his brother Max, would see of him. The problem they had at the time was the pace of their lives, working day and night, there was very little time for anything else, and Max had married Beryl and children dominated any time they had off. It was during this period that Max first had the incentive and of course contacts, to create and develop wrestling stars himself.

One of them was Ronnie "Ace" Allcard from Sheffield, who was interviewed during the writing of this book, but sadly died in September 2012. He first met the Crabtree brothers in the 1960s, after being introduced by a fighter called Jack Harris, who had the reputation as one of the hardest fighting men in the country. Nevertheless he took Ace under his wing, but it took him a few years to get fights because he was always scrapping outside of the ring. Once Max introduced him to George de Relwyskow (who was running Scotland for Joint) he started to give Ace regular bouts. Later, when Max took charge of the territory, things really started to take off for Ace; and he described Shirley as a powerful, boisterous fighter, who was a lovely man and good a listener too.

There were those who did not like him, but Shirley couldn't care less about any of them, and he treated them with the same contempt he had shown to Bert Assirati, and the Sergeant Majors in the Coldstream Guards who had tried to boss him about. He knew who his friends were and the rest could go run and jump. There were many wrestlers who liked to just talk, but Shirley listened too. If you had him as a friend, he was a very strong ally, and Ace spent time with him training, and going on runs across the Yorkshire moors with his bull terriers.

Tag team wrestling started to become well-liked in the UK in the early 1960s. It had been going on in America for a number of years, and now British stars such as the Royal Brothers, the Black Diamonds, and the Silent Ones were becoming very popular. Shirley started to team up with Max, and they had a few bouts, but he would come to regard Jackie Turpin and Mal Sanders as his favourite tag partners. While he was still in his prime he was seen mainly in singles matches, and it is only when he lost his conditioning and piled on the weight as Big Daddy, that he became known for appearing almost exclusively in tag team matches. He would team up with younger, fitter fighters who would do most of the work, and then he would come in and finish the fight off with a couple of belly butts, and the famous Daddy-splash.

There are a lot of stories surrounding this era, and a lot of wrestlers and journalists have pointed out that Shirley's performances were extremely limited, but that is not what it was about. This was an era of showmanship, where his entrance sometimes lasted longer than the fighting he did in the ring. When people turn up to see film stars and singers making public appearances they do not suddenly expect them to burst into song, they just want to see them in the flesh. By using his brother for just a few minutes a night, Max was able to extend his career into the 1990s, although the critics point to the damage this caused to wrestling's reputation, and of course, to Shirley himself. Undoubtedly, Daddy's fights did become stale and repetitive come the end, and with 25 years of hindsight it is easy to pick them apart. The fact was, having the name "Big Daddy" at the top of the bill was what drew in the crowd, and if you had been there in one of those packed halls you would have experienced an electric atmosphere reminiscent of an international football match with the sound of air-horns all around.

The British Wrestling Federation had originally been created by independent promoters to allow Assirati to continue claiming the crown, but of course, his brutal style, coupled with the fact that he refused to lose, was why Joint got the hump with him. There are so many stories surrounding this era, and a lot of it cannot be substantiated. As we have already mentioned, Bert did try to heckle Shirley at least once. He had done a similar thing to Lou Thesz at the Royal Albert Hall where he stood up and mocked him in front of the crowd, but Shirley was not going to take that. When Assirati tried to do the same thing to him he simply walked out, whatever beef Assirati had with the bosses was nothing to do with him.

From 1960, wrestling started to be broadcast every Saturday afternoon, and this is when fighters really started to become household names, although Shirley never appeared on TV back then as he wasn't working for Joint. Assirati was known as a shooter, but this had nothing to do with guns or sex. In the wrestling world a shooter is a fighter who has the ability to launch unscripted attacks on his opponent, and Bert was pretty good at that. Many people say in a straight contest between the two men Assirati would have had the upper hand, but Shirley was in his prime then and he would have certainly given him a run for his money, and may well have come away with a victory in a fair and even contest. Granted, Assirati was as strong as an ox, but Shirley had immense power even when he got to Bert's age.

The late 1950s and early 1960s really was a golden era for wrestling, which drew in big crowds as a new fan base was created by the television shows. With such an audience to cater for, Joint Promotions were all over the place, and many of their nights were sold out. It was a very basic formula; you had a goodie, and a baddie, who broke the rules and hurt his opponent. A tussle would then ensue, and this could go on for months, possibly years, across many towns and cities. There was a certain amount of naivety in the audiences, but when you are told something was real, and you can see its stomach flopping around in front of you, you tended to believe it.

In the 21st century we have soap opera; people sit in any of the endless amount of coffee shops on one of the soulless high streets of Britain, all huddled together supping brews and chatting rubbish. You hear it at bus stops, on trains and in Post Offices, they slip terrible news in between tales of personal ailments, hip replacements, and ASDA's two-for-one offers on brisket and corned beef. They talk of murder, rape, battery and abuse like they are personally involved, or their neighbour is a reincarnation of Fred West. In the end, it all turns out to be a storyline from *EastEnders*, or *Coronation Street*, but there is real venom in their voice as their flu jab kick-in and blurs the line between truth and fiction. Wrestling worked that way too; the same kinds of people got tangled up in its storylines and plots. The only difference was that they really believed what they saw in the ring was genuine and true for a long while.

> *"There's a magic to it [wrestling] – it's very, very basic… It goes back to even the youngest childhood of cowboys and indians, and in our lives, we never grow out of that. As long as there's a good baddie and a good goodie, there will always be business… The people like to see the goodie coming back and winning the fight, when earlier they saw him being pummelled against the ropes and looking like losing the contest."*

The story goes that Shirley's first wife Marilyn Kelly left him. Whether they drifted apart or their personalities clashed is hard to tell and depends on who you talk to. What is for sure is that he ended up having one hell of a time of it. In the beginning they were a good couple; Marilyn was a pretty girl who would sometimes come to the fights and help with the tickets and various other jobs that needed to be done. Max found his brother's divorce hard to take, but the truth is it was nothing to do with him. Part of the reason he felt this way was because of the closeness they had back then and he shared in his grief. It took him a little while to accept Shirley back into the fold in the beginning because the Crabtrees did not split with their wives, it was one of the unwritten rules which stopped them from being like their father.

By his own admission, Shirley always fell for dominant women, but the problem with two dominant characters is there is often a conflict. As the years rolled on Shirley certainly mellowed, and he lost the tepidity of his youth. As his fame increased his private life became quieter and more family orientated. At the beginning of the 1960s, there were a lot of things bubbling away under the surface and he wasn't afforded the luxury and comfort of his later life. Money was tight, and there wasn't just the wrestling to concentrate on; they had their other business interests too. A lot of hard work still lay ahead, and this was the beginning of a very long journey which saw Shirley's transformation from an obscure heel into the mega-face of the 1970s and 1980s.

It was a journey which lasted over 40 years for Shirley, and it took him right across the lands of Great Britain and beyond. Travelling the highways and byways, he knew many of them like the back of his hand, and they would always try to be back for a late supper just to say they were home. Sometimes they slept in the backs of their cars, or out under the stars using their kitbags as pillows. They saw all the grotty guest houses from Aberdeen to St Ives. Some had decent beds; others knocked up a nice bit of breakfast, with as many mushrooms as you liked just as long as you didn't mind scraping them off of the back of the toilet house door.

They had been cooped up in Rhonddan doss houses full of miners watching *Dixon of Dock Green* with the volume up way to high. They had even shared red plastic tomatoes full of ketchup with Geordie truckers in transport cafés outside of Skegness, and it was all in the name of business. They had slept top-to-toe in the back of vans, and caravans in all types of weather just so the show could go on. The 1960s was a great time to be alive, but didn't they graft just to get a footing. Gradually, their willingness, contacts, and developing business acumen put the Crabtree brothers in among it all just at the right time. None of the men running Joint were spring chickens, and in time they would look for younger blood to carry on.

On 9 February 1961, the Beatles performed their first gig at the Cavern Club in Liverpool, but it didn't even get a mention in a new publication called the *Sunday Telegraph*. Further north, at the Workington Opera House, you would have been able to see "the golden boy of wrestling" Max Crabtree in action against Londoner Tommy Holton if you fancied it, and he was going great guns at this point in time. At three, five, or seven pence a seat, it was not as cheap a night out as it could have been, but if you didn't have a bird to take to the pictures it was better than sitting at home amusing yourself with just two television channels and a dog-eared copy of the *Tiger*.

BBC Two was just around the corner; it was launched in April 1964, but things didn't quite go to plan. A massive fire at Battersea Power Station meant that the original launch had to be postponed despite an offer from the opposition to help, which "Auntie" politely rejected. None of this affected the wrestling of course, which was doing really well on ITV, and this was what angered many of Joint's wrestlers who were appearing regularly. The money was just as bad on the TV as it was outside of the cartel, and after winning the European heavyweight title in 1961, Shirley quit the BWF.

In March, Shirley fought Big Boy Scott at the Lancaster Baths and Gargantua at Granby Halls, Leicester, in May. Also on the bill were both of his brothers, and it appeared Shirley and Brian recorded victories whilst Max was knocked out by Tommy Holton in a junior heavyweight contest. On Friday 30 June, Shirley then fought Roy "Bull" Davies in London in what was billed as a terrific heavyweight clash, and there was also a separate eight-man knockout contest boasting the likes of Bobby Barnes and Ken Joyce.

For a fight against Bill Coverdale, it was necessary to reinforce the ring to make things absolutely safe as their combined weight was 50st, and this fight took place in Edgware Road in July. After a while, the feeling that he was beginning to tread water started to creep in on Shirley and maybe working for so many independents wasn't doing him any good. Being billed as British and European heavyweight champion always drew a crowd, but he felt he could become a bigger name and earn decent money, and in time he was proven to be right. It would of course be through TV exposure that this finally happened for him, but for a while he just fought locally and made himself a bigger name on a smaller scale and as we've mentioned, this made his life a lot less hectic, although he did still do bits and pieces across the country.

Paul Lincoln's signing of Mike Marino was seen as another threat by the head honchos at Joint, who were now starting to really take notice of him, and of course Max because of the way he ran his wrestling shows. The early 1960s were also the peak of Max's wrestling career, and he got close to taking the British lightweight title a couple of times. His style was described as "continental" with lots of backdrops, dives off ropes, flying tackles and drop-kicks, which left the audience breathless. He also had a natural flair for sports presentation, which was the side of the ropes he was starting to lean towards, and when Joint offered him the opportunity to work for them in 1962, he jumped at the chance.

On 2 January 1962, BBC One broadcasted its first episode of the pioneering police drama *Z Cars*. Set in the fictional village of Newtown on the outskirts of Liverpool it was seen as a more realistic interpretation of policing during those days, like the more recent series *Heartbeat* has tried to recapture in a far more rural setting. A couple of days later, and still unknown, four other Liverpudlians were on the prowl. The Beatles played on their very first album; the song was called 'My Bonnie', and it was credited to Tony Sheridan and the Beat Boys and released by Polydor. Nobody could have predicted the phenomenal rise the Fab Four would make the following year, and while they were of course a very talented group, like the Crabtrees they were the right people, in the right place, at the right time. They had talent, and were cunning enough to be able to spin a thick enough line of bull to get their ticket to ride.

Their big break came at the end of 1963, and the intergalactic success really began the following year, which was also around the time Jack Harris (who wrestled as the Plymouth Rock) broke his neck in the ring and was forced to quit. Like Brian Crabtree (whose career ended with a broken leg) Jack ended up refereeing for Max, and he became a member of the background team. Brian's accident happened at the Caledonian baths, where the brothers battled three Hungarians, with Brian fighting a lightweight, Max a middleweight, and Shirley pitted against the biggest of the three. When Brian got hurt Shirley had to carry him over his shoulder to the ambulance, and he swore to them that he would never wrestle again.

There was another big contest for Shirley in Tooting at Granada's showpiece theatre working for Paul Lincoln Promotions a couple of times. It was here as Dr Death that Lincoln had his momentous match with the White Angel, and he hoped such shows would be enough to change the power base in British wrestling. On the programme Shirley was recognised as the British champion and in a bout billed as "The Battle of True Giants", he fought Big Bill Coverdale. Lincoln and his team almost secured a midweek spot on *World of Sport*, but instead it went to Joint, and many feel the difference in the style of Lincoln's match-making would have really added something to the televised coverage but it wasn't to be. The Crabtrees' domination of wrestling was still a decade away, and Shirley would drift into relative obscurity with his best fighting years behind him before that. When he did return, he was bigger than ever in fame as well as size, as he took on the persona of Big Daddy, the people's champion.

Chapter Six

Try And Catch The Wind

NO LONGER hanging about on Blackpool beach in his Speedos, the early 1960s was when Shirley first started to spend his summers in Neumarkt, Vienna, wrestling at promoter George Blemenschutz's famous tournaments. It was better than sitting under the pier eating way too many cockles and waiting for the rain to ease up, and it certainly beat rescuing drunken revellers from the sea, and there wasn't a kiss-me-quick hat to be seen for a least a thousand miles.

Vienna is a land we fondly associate with apfelstrudel, wiener schnitzel, Christmas markets, and snow, a city whose citizens hold a deep-seated feeling of loss since the all-singing, all-dancing Von Trapp family cleared off to Switzerland to escape the Nazis during the Second World War. They would return, or their film counter parts would, while the real Von Trapps moved to America and lived the high life. Famous musical writers Rodgers and Hammerstein got actress Julie Andrews and her mates to high-tail it across to Austria to re-enact the drama for a film which was a massive success, and Julie really belted out the songs. Once again, the hills were alive, which scared mountain-grazing livestock into the edelweiss.

The Sound of Music was finally released in 1965, and Shirley would later take his family to see some of the beautiful locations used in the film.

Drawing in crowds of at least 8,000, six or seven nights a week, the Neumarkt bouts were a good place to pit your wits if you were outside the Joint cartel, and many British wrestlers fought out there against grapplers from Europe and other parts of the world. Slurl (as George Blemenschutz was known to his mates) was nicknamed the "Neumarkt Mummy" because of his age, and he fought his last bout at 70, which surpassed Shirley's age in his final contest by seven years. Teaming up with Tony Stewart, Shirley's health was not good at that point, and his participation was brief. In Margate in 1993, he finally brought the curtain down on a career which lasted 41 years, and if the truth be known his performances as Big Daddy were seven or eight years past their best.

Nevertheless, the early 1960s was an exciting period for him, and the time he spent out in Vienna made him fall in love with the place. He was used to fighting in all manner of locations, be it some scruffy barn with straw on the floor to soak up the piss, or in a grand old Victorian Hall in the middle of a town centre. Viennese crowds were different, and it sometimes felt like they were on the verge of rioting themselves. Fighting in front of such large audiences was really something, and a taste of what was to come. There was lots of time off between bouts which dragged for some of the lads. Being fond of the great outdoors Shirley went and saw it all, and when he wasn't out walking, he was training at Vienna University, and also helped to coach the amateur wrestling squad.

By 1963, Bob Sweeney had pretty much made up his mind that he was finished with the world of wrestling, and he quit the following year to pursue his own business interests. He had seen Shirley slow things up a little to concentrate on business, and being a man he admired, he sought his advice. At the time, both wrestlers were working outside of Joint, and they realised there wasn't a great deal of money to be made. Besides which, there were a lot of old pros about, and seeing them ringside with their walking sticks was enough to put anybody off, and all of this registered with Bob.

What had happened to Jack Harris was a stark reminder that life was short, and if you stayed in the wrestling game for any great period of time, whatever was left of your shattered body when you retired could be poured quite easily into the nearest care home. With Max's business mind, Shirley's inspiration, and younger brother Brian thinking on his feet, the brothers were regularly promoting dances, pop bands, and wrestling shows as well as wrestling themselves, and they had attracted some of the biggest recording artists in the business to the north. Bob's own business idea involved gymnasiums. The problem as far as he could see was the fact that bodybuilding was a pretty specialist hobby in Britain at the time and there was a gap in the market as Shirley remembered:

> "England was nothing like America, and Bob wanted to emulate the clubs over there by opening a gym which would be pleasant to train in. He also wanted it to be the kind of place which was accessible to the everyday working man, who might like to come in after work, or maybe at the weekend, as well as the professional sportsman. One of the issues he faced was from coaches, who still believed bodybuilding was detrimental to a training regime, all they ever saw were competition bodybuilders who could be cumbersome; they didn't realise that there was more to it than that, and that's why none of your professionals were using weights back then. He put up with a lot of stick over that, but we were right in what we were saying – all you had to do was look at what was going on in America. Bob was always a very forward-thinking man, and I have to take my hat off to him; he did absolutely fantastic."

Having found premises to rent, Bob took Shirley to have a look at what was essentially a big room right in the heart of Halifax. By the 1960s, many of the mills had been closed and office space was in abundance, and it didn't cost the earth. As Shirley took great strides into the room, Bob explained his vision to him. After he had finished speaking, Shirley threw open the big window at the end, and he looked out across the town with its mills, smoking chimneys, and the moors beyond with a real sense of freedom. With the wind rustling his blonde locks, he had his moment of clarity, which ended with one of his famous smiles.

Bob recalls that he almost always had a very calm demeanour, and he would sometimes have defining moments, or inspire others, which was another side of his personality which was very much different to characters he portrayed in the ring. All wrestlers have to become a kind of Jekyll and Hyde type of character, with the crowd just seeing their alter ego. Only in the dressing room would you see the "personal" side of a bunch of boisterous wrestlers psyching themselves up as they slipped out of their y-fronts and into their shiny spandex leotards. The familiar aroma of Old Spice, Brut and stale sweat would soon fill Bob's gym as his venture began, but he would always remember Shirley staring out of that window, watching the great big nimbus cumulus as they rolled in across the dales. He told him that he could see for miles and miles, and it was almost like he could see into the future; which for Shirley, turned out to be orange.

Or at least the car was that he bought in the mid-1970s when he had made his money, and it was probably the only luxury he ever afforded himself. Big Daddy Crabtree cruised around the country in a burnt orange Granada Mark II with a brown leather roof.

While Bob quickly became established and made his fortune, it took Shirley a while longer. Just when he thought it was all over and he was sliding into obscurity, Big Daddy erupted on to the scene via the screens of the nation and became the rotund Yorkshireman everybody loved. Even Margaret Thatcher sent a message asking for his autograph, and the Queen kicked off her slippers and curled up on the sofa with a Wedgwood full of tea to watch him on a Saturday afternoon on more than one occasion.

In the fullness of time, what Shirley said to Bob about seeing for miles has taken on prophetical properties when you consider what the two men went on to achieve in their individual careers.

You can't help but picture the big man speeding down country lanes, filling up the whole of the drivers' side of the car as he made his way to the next show, which would be filled with thousands of his fans all waiting to see, all wanting to touch. With one tracksuited arm and five chubby digits hanging out of the window, and Matt Monroe on the eight-track, you can almost see him disappearing off into the distance like a fiery orange comet for hundreds of miles until he arrived with his carnival show in the next town.

Places like Blackpool, Morecambe, Cleethorpes, and Brighton. The posters were usually bright yellow, or green, sometimes red, and they advertised the show with tall black letters, which spelled out his name (and who he was going to defeat next) at the top of the bill. There would be a picture of him holding a baby, or striking a pose, and they were plastered across billboards and subways from Land's End to John o'Groats in a land where Thatcher was God, and the devil was a Sex Pistol.

If the sight of Shirley was iconic, then Bob was revolutionary in more practical terms. He changed people's opinions about bodybuilding, and he inspired many to start up their own clubs. Today, plush health clubs and gyms have sprung up all over Great Britain but Bob was the first, and he drew his inspiration from his friend. Indeed, Bob's rugby coach, like many others, was of the opinion that weight training actually slowed a person down, so Shirley and Bob were early educators against this belief. There was no recognition that the correct body building programme could make an athlete faster, but today you would be hard pushed to find a professional sportsman who did not do some form of weight training.

There were those who made negative remarks to Bob, and for years he felt like he was fighting a losing battle, but gradually his fitness ideas started to take hold. As a boy, Shirley's rugby coach told him he needed to get bigger. He didn't have a clue how he could enhance his size until he started to read the American bodybuilding magazines, and of course he came across that picture of Eugene Sandow. All the Crabtree brothers did a lot of swimming which helped to develop their physiques, but looking back it is very difficult to see from today's perspective how people did not cotton on to these training methods earlier.

Bob was certainly a pioneer in this country, but Shirley encouraged him to take things forward if he wanted to emulate people like Reg Park and Spencer Churchill. Worried about what the lads would get up to, Bob's mother would never let him follow Max and Shirley to Blackpool to go life guarding during those summer months. He would always be in awe of their bronzed and muscular physiques when they returned at the end of the season, and he decided he wanted to develop his own body.

Knowing he had the business experience of the Crabtrees to call on if he needed it, Bob put his heart and soul into his business. Still only a young man, he knew it was now or never and he made a real go of it. As a wrestler Bob has often been mentioned in the same breath as master technicians Eric Taylor and Ernie Riley, but the fact that he retired at 30 (seven years after his debut) means than many people missed out on seeing him on TV.

Most towns did have gyms, but they were unwelcoming and you had to be highly dedicated if you were going to keep in shape. Bob's plan was to broaden the concept of the gymnasium, and he also included other aspects of a healthy lifestyle. Although Shirley wasn't the only person he talked to he was certainly one of the most enthusiastic, although Bradford wrestler Don Branch did champion his cause. Every year, professional wrestlers came over from America on tour and this is how Bob met George Bolas, the Zebra Kid, who was OK with how things were done in the States.

He had worked as a manager in a health club over there, and he knew all about anatomy, nutrition, and physiology and he inspired Bob to educate himself. He also taught him about the art of selling knowing only too well that he would have to go out and flog gym memberships if he was going to be a success, which was something Bob hadn't even considered. Bob put himself on a Dale Carnegie selling course almost straight away and gradually he spread the word, and he ended up with a chain of a dozen health centres spread across the UK as people started to cotton on to his idea. When Shirley next came down to check on Bob's progress, he brought Jack Wilkinson and Welsh rugby player John Thorley with him to see what it was all about. Bob managed to get them training regularly with weights and they both went on to play at international level.

In November 1963, just a couple of weeks after Jim Breaks won the first of many British lightweight championships, and Johnny Kwango ("The King of Head-Butts") did the Royal show, news of the death of President Kennedy was filtering through to the United Kingdom.

Britain had its own problems; somebody was abducting children around Shirley's way, and doors and windows were starting to be locked at night. On 23 November, the night that a new science-fiction show called *Doctor Who* was first shown on the BBC, Myra Hindley and Ian Brady abducted a 12-year-old boy called John Kilbride from a market in Ashton-under-Lyne, which was only 20 miles from Halifax. It seemed like nobody was safe after dark, and for a while evening attendances dwindled at many of the cinemas, bingo halls and nightclubs, but the Crabtrees were largely unaffected. There was a pair of psychos using Yorkshire as their hunting ground, and bodies would later turn up on Saddleworth Moor which was an area Shirley sometimes used to train and walk. There had been scares before, but nothing like this had been seen in Yorkshire in living memory. In total, the Moors Murderers would claim five known victims, with only three bodies being recovered. This was just the beginning of their killing spree which went on until October 1965, just as Britain was abolishing the death sentence for murder, and they received life sentences after their trials the following year.

The end of 1963 saw a quiet family Christmas for the Crabtrees and they enjoyed some relaxation time after a busy period. There was a new lady in Shirley's life, which gave him a lift, and things were once again looking good for the future. On the final Saturday before Christmas there was televised wrestling from Willesden, and a tag match between The Royals and The Black Diamonds was what the crowd had come to see.

On Boxing Day, as people settled down for the Queen's speech, things were going crazy in America once again. With the death of Kennedy there had been a time of mourning, businesses had been shut down over the weekend the President had been killed, and something was needed to cheer up the nation and revive the American dream. The Yanks went absolutely mental when the Beatles released 'I Want To Hold Your Hand', which is something Al Nicol may well have been whispering to southern area welterweight champion Mick McManus as he twisted his scrotum up around the back of his neck in the last televised wrestling of the year from Seymour Hall.

Eight miles away, in Tottenham, there was decent trade at the Batsford chip shop and Mick may well have been thinking about pie, chips and mushy peas as he slipped out of Al Nicols's hold and went in for the kill. If he did go via Tottenham on the way home, he would not have been guaranteed a queue jump despite his status. Instead, he would have had to stand in line with a load of suicidal Spurs fans who had just seen their team get battered by West Bromwich Albion. They never did do the league and cup double again, and they ultimately lost out to Everton in the race to the title that year.

In early 1964, the idea of the Channel Tunnel first came into the public consciousness, and it was expected to be completed by 1969, but the concept did not become a reality until November 1994. Stretching from Coquelles in Calais to Folkestone in Kent, it fast became the most popular way into Britain if you did not have a passport.

On 30 March 1964, on Clacton Beach in Essex, it was handbags at dawn as it all kicked off between the Mods and the Rockers. Labelled by the popular press as "Folk Devils" there was a hell of a punch-up, which the police struggled to deal with. A popular seaside venue, Shirley wrestled in Clacton-on-Sea on many occasions, and perhaps the sight of a load of wrestlers bounding up the beach in full regalia may just have been surreal enough to stop the kids fighting, but I doubt it. And who were the crowd-pullers in the ring that year? Shirley certainly wasn't a big star on a national scale, but he did have quite a following locally. Besides Mick McManus, other wrestlers topping the bill included Earl Maynard, Jack Dempsey, George Kidd, and Albert Wall, but none of them were bigger news than the Great Train Robbers, who stole £2.6m (the equivalent of £40m in today's money) and the judge threw the book at them that year. It was also the year that a friend of Shirley's, the Reverend Michael Brooks, swapped the pulpit for the ring. A fully ordained Methodist minister, he would appear in Shirley's corner on more than one occasion, and it caused quite a stir when he first started wrestling. It was however one hell of a gimmick and he swept away his fair share of sinners.

Wayne Bridges was also in the news as he stepped up towards stardom after fighting as an amateur for five years. He became another jewel in Paul Lincoln's crown as he unsuccessfully challenged Joint for the ITV contract, which kept them in control of British wrestling.

On Bonfire Night 1964, Shirley tagged with Max once again, this time in Edinburgh, and they beat Bruno Elrington and Stoker Morris a few days before the bill went through the House of Commons to abolish the death sentence, with the last execution taking place in August.

Another Halifax lad causing a splash that year was wrestler Farmer Johnny Allan. After turning professional in 1951, he beat Norman Walsh in 1964 to take the British mid-heavyweight title. In November, Petula Clark's hit single 'Downtown' entered the charts at number 41, just as Kendo Nagasaki was making his debut against Jumping Jim Hussey. 'Downtown' ended up getting to number two come Christmas, kept off the top of the stack by the Beatles, and by then Shirley had married local lass Sally Greenwood in Halifax. A pretty girl with short black hair, in the wedding photo Shirley towers over her as they stand in the church doorway. Looking every inch like wrestlers and businessmen, he has one arm draped causally around his new bride, while Max is stood beside him looking like a Teddy Boy with his hands thrust deeply into his pockets. This time Shirley hoped he had finally found the right girl; little did he know there was more heartbreak to follow for both brothers.

All of the Crabtrees' efforts paid off when they were able to secure a lease on premises in Halifax which they turned into Big Daddies nightclub, and it opened on 24 March 1964:

> *"We went on and opened Big Daddies Club at the site that used to be the Collinson's café which was a couple of streets away from the Marlborough Hall, where we had been putting on Friday and Saturday night dances. The premises were on the upper floors of a building at the top of Crown Street, and it was here that Donovan performed [on 15 May 1965]. We also invited him to town to open our new clothes shop The In Crowd in Westgate. There was a massive crowd in Crown Street, and the police got hold of us because they were worried he would get mobbed, and I must admit we were worried ourselves. Bringing such a star to Halifax was a major event, and we had to go to the White Swan Hotel to collect him… We went to the second floor and into Donovan's room, and there he was draped across the bed with that silly little hat on… We said we had to leave now on police advice to go to Big Daddies but when we got to the outside door, it was heaving with people. We all went out behind Big Tony [a doorman] who was 6ft 7in in his*

stocking feet but when he saw the size of the crowd, he grabbed Donovan and slung him over his shoulder… Well Donovan lost his cap and his shoes in the chaos… Inside the club the police inspector said we had to get a car and get Donovan away from the area… they bundled Donovan into the back. Well, there were kids on the bonnet as we shot up Crown Street; it was like a Wild West show. Donovan wasn't allowed to go back into town, so he never opened the shop."

Chapter Seven

There's Only One Dickie Davies

I T WASN'T until the autumn of 1965 that wrestling went full-time on ITV as part of the new *World of Sport* programme. Originally hosted by Eamonn Andrews, who, as we know, really established himself as a household name with *This Is Your Life*, when he was out there in front of the cameras stringing all of those sports stories into one cohesive whole, there was another man with such expertise waiting in the wings. Every picture you can conjure in your mind of the quintessential 1970s sports presenter stops at this man's door. The drone of the football results, the smell of bubble and squeak, mashing tea, and the metallic clunk of the wrestling bell as the rain pelts down outside.

All of these memories were etched on our minds, coming to us via cathode rays from television sets across the nation. Imprinting their electrons into our minds were visions of huge grapplers as they stopped at the bell between rounds with the camera pointing up at them from the apron. Heads throbbing, pulses racing, and blood pressures surpassing 160 over 100, they heaved in great lungfuls and waited for their opponent to come at them again in red, white, and blue spandex or crumpled corduroy. Almost all of these memories from an era long gone are embodied in just one man, and he brought it all together in a rather less Gaelic fashion than his predecessor.

Whether it was the crisp tweed, or the soft tones of yellow and brown (which made him look like a banana) who knows? Cool but casual, with the quiff and the porn star moustache, he spoke like somebody was holding his nose, but he was, in fact, a legend. We have to of course honour Eamonn, and thank him for what he did, but everything that lives and breathes *World of Sport*, from Shergar to Haystacks, Nick Faldo to Jocky Wilson, all revolves around the memory of one man. There was indeed only one Dickie Davies.

In actual fact there have been a couple of famous people called Dickie Davies, but the one we are concentrating on here could have been Bert Reynolds's half-brother. Born in Wallasey, Merseyside, in April 1933, after Grammar School and National Service, he started out as an announcer on Southern Television, and he only started to call himself "Dickie" professionally after pundit and former football player Jimmy Hill told him to. Dickie started as Eamonn's understudy; if the jovial Irishman's evening ended up with him drunk and not getting up in the morning, or if he simply had other commitments, Davies was the man who stepped it. When Andrews quit in 1968, Dickie was his natural successor, and while Eamonn crossed the divide from sport to *This Is Your Life* rather well, Davies forged his own place in sporting television history. His face popping up throughout a rain-swept Saturday afternoon made you feel safe. It confirmed that the wrestling had ended, and Saturday night was finally here, and you would soon be flicking over to the BBC for *Dixon of Dock Green*.

Despite the gathering peace movement, the mid-1960s was a scary time to be alive, especially if you were living in the East End of London. In early January 1965, the Kray twins were still running their Bethnal Green manor, and you certainly didn't mess with them. Ronnie and Reggie were then arrested for running a protection racket in London, but they didn't go to the nick; they continued merrily terrorising people for a couple more years. They were arguably the biggest gangsters in Britain during the 1950s and 1960s, and were involved in many robberies and even a couple of murders. They were also in the nightclub game, but thankfully, the Crabtrees never had any dealings with them. Instead, they kept to the right side of the law and the respect they were paid came through hard work and not fear. It wasn't until 1968 that the Krays were permanently taken off the streets when they were arrested for the murder of Jack "The Hat" McVitie.

The Krays' and the Crabtrees' lives and upbringings were very similar. Both sets of lads had very tough mothers, but the Crabtrees had been ingrained with a strong sense of what was right and wrong. In fact her words hung around in his mind all his life, and back then, if he ever was tempted to stray from the path of righteousness, she would soon beat the wrongness out of him:

> "My mum weighed 15st. Her dad had been a black-smith, and she used to strike the hammer. She had tremendous arms on her; she could carry a hundred-weight of coal up six flights of stairs. I know it doesn't sound very feminine, but I have always liked women who are strong in every possible way. She worked from seven in the morning until half-past five at night, really grafted to give us lads a good start in life."

It was true that nobody working-class had anything of any real value back then. If there had been PlayStations, plasma TVs, and dishwashers, there is no way people would have left their doors open at night back in the good old days. The little people did have, they grafted for. The Crabtrees were strong enough to muscle their way into these sorts of shady worlds if they had wanted to, but they were not that way inclined. They knew there was a proper and decent way to conduct themselves and their lives, and although they were not overly religious, they were God-fearing men. At the end of January 1965, Winston Churchill's funeral took place, and if they had ever needed a reminder of how to fight through terrifying odds and win through, then all they had to do was think of Churchill smoking a fat cigar and doing the two-fingered "V for victory" salute.

The brothers were delighted to acquire the services of Lulu and The Luvvers on 27 February 1965, just after 'Shout' had hit the number eight position in the British hit parade. It cost six shillings to get into Big Daddies that night, and the Halifax crowd were treated to what was described by the local paper as: "A performance that was so dynamic and full of movement that it left even the fittest among the sell-out crowd absolutely exhausted."

They had a local discotheque firm providing the light and sound, and they stuck one of their guys on Lulu's door to make sure no riff-raff got in to see the Scottish star. Her hair was bright orange and many of the female fans who met her were left wondering what hair products she had used. Lonnie Cook's band The Kandymen sometimes played Big Daddies, and he recalls what was different about Shirley's club was the volume; he would always be asking the sound guys to turn it up, and they got in a guy from the local hi-fi shop to rig up the whole of the side of the stage with speakers.

Because they played records so loud, any band that followed the disco had to give it some welly just to keep the audience pumped up. Not only was Big Daddies the place to be seen, it was the scene, and it was the loudest venue in town. Shirley and Brian used to love to get up into the middle of the stage and play records, although of course, there were resident DJs. This was a peak time for The Kandymen, who were playing sometimes six or seven nights a week and Lonnie remembers going into the back office of the club to pick up his money one night and looking like death warmed up. Shirley was sat behind the desk all business like, and was staring at Lonnie's black, sleep-deprived eyes. He looked like Alice Cooper, or a member of the rock band Kiss, way before The Crazy World of Arthur Brown first portrayed that kind of look in the video to their single 'Fire'. Shirley turned to Lonnie and told him he needed to get more rest, eat good foods, and look after himself, which is rather ironic when we think of all of those decades he would spend on the road doing much the same thing and ignoring his own advice.

On another occasion, The Kandymen were coming off stage at the Marlborough Hall only to be greeted by Shirley who asked them to do the late session at Big Daddies club up the road. The band they had booked had dropped out at the last moment and they didn't have an act, so Lonnie and his chums ended up doing a second stint. The only problem was that the club did not have a piano so Shirley, assisted by members of the band and a couple of doormen, picked up the one they had been using in the hall, and they carried it through the streets until they got to the club. With Shirley shouting "the show must go on!" at the top of his voice, it was a scene reminiscent of the Laurel and Hardy film *The Music Box*, where they carry a piano up many steps to a house. They were all erupting into fits of laughter and trying not to drop the thing, and then they had to make their way through a crowd of dancing teenagers and up yet more stairs to the stage.

The brothers went on to have a number of good years at the club, and at the other locations they put on nights, and it didn't start to fizzle out until the latter part of the 1960s, when they sold the club to Paul Mountain who changed the name to Clarence's. Paul remembers that the brothers had had enough of running the club by then, attendances had started to drop, and they'd tried to change the image a few times calling it the 2 + 2 Club, and The Scene. After a brief meeting, Paul bought the lease from them and this signalled the end of their full-time association with the nightclub scene. Their clothes shop The In Crowd also died a death despite boasting the latest fashions straight from Carnaby Street. This was in fact the problem; the people of Halifax were not ready for such high fashion and the shop soon closed down.

Shirley was teaming up with various tag team partners, including his brothers, and in August they faced the Campbell brothers, Angus and Jock. By the mid-1960s, the promoters operating under the umbrella of booking engine Joint Promotions had doubled the amount of live shows they were doing, and were now putting on around 4,500 a year, and every town of note had at least one show a month. It was a huge operation, with more than 30 cities having a weekly show.

Max was now running Scotland, and he fast built a reputation for success. By the late 1960s, he had tried his hand at promoting a lot of things, and even at this stage it was looking like he was going to have a bigger say in the way things were run at Joint. Down south, for Dale Martins, Mick McManus was doing much the same thing as Max, although continuing to wrestle himself was very much at the forefront of his mind. The man everybody loved to hate in the ring was always top of the bill, and usually the first name people recall when they talk about televised wrestling in the 1950s and 1960s. Mick became the main booker in the London area, and such was his fame he released his own book in 1970. With the full force of Dale Martin's publicity machine behind him he even went on to flog his own pep-pills, and he was hip enough to hang out with the Beatles, despite the fact he celebrated his 50th birthday in 1971.

On the independent circuit, top wrestler Orig Williams went off to fight in India, Pakistan, the Far East and Mexico, where he adopted the nickname "El Bandito" because of his handle-bar moustache. The Welshman was a physically imposing character who believed in hard matches, and on his return he offered further competition to Joint's operation when he started to seriously promote, and on his books he had wrestlers such as Adrian Street, The Mighty John Quinn, Mark Rocco, and Johnny Saint.

On 7 March 1965, racial tensions boiled over in the US's own version of Bloody Sunday. In Selma, Alabama, 200 state troopers clashed with over 500 protesters and they beat them with clubs. The civil rights movement was well underway but there was much tension in America at the time, and Lindon B. Johnson sending more troops into Vietnam didn't help matters.

In the summer, as Great Train Robber Ronnie Biggs was doing a bunk over Wandsworth Prison wall into a removal van, Shirley found himself at home with the wife and a new baby boy called Lionel. He could still be seen doing shows around Blackpool for Cyril Knowles, and he used a couple of different gimmicks, and even fought in a mask as "White Angel" as a whole set of fresh tensions crept into the marriage.

Paul Lincoln had strong links with the Parisian wrestling scene at the time, and it was he who first brought in the tag team Les Blousons Noirs (The Black Jackets). In return, Lincoln let some of his lads wrestle in Paris. At the time, the TV show *The Untouchables* was still very popular, and the Parisians fed off such imagery. With their leather jackets they were unliked by British fans, who dubbed them "The French Teddy Boys". They fought against wrestlers such as Ken Joyce and Eddie Capelli, and the Cortez Brothers, and at the end of the decade, they returned to Britain to wrestle for Joint. Afterwards, when they once again returned to Paris, they took Max's wife Beryl and Shirley's wife Sally with them as lovers.

By then Shirley's daughter Catherine had been born, but his was a life largely without those children, and for a while the Crabtree lads felt like the walls were coming in on them. One thing they did have was resilience, which led them on to a golden period in the mid-to-late 1970s, and they ended up running professional wrestling for well over a decade. After the wives had left, Max decided to high-tail it across to Paris to bring Beryl back, but Shirley had other ideas. Sally had made her bed and she could lie in it. If that was what she wanted, then that is what she would have, but in truth, he was heart broken to lose his wife and children, but there was no way he was having her back. Twice he had trusted, and twice he had been hurt.

For a while, he was out in the wilderness as his whole world turned upside down. It was then that he began to pile on the weight, losing his boyish good looks and becoming the more loveable figure that millions grew to know and love. There was no disguising the fact that he had been hurt by Sally but, like he often told others, the show must go on and that is exactly what happened. Other promotions companies were suddenly nipping at Joint's heels and, in an inspired move, they staved off the threat by merging with Paul Lincoln's organisation:

"As the years passed I think I can say I continued to hold my own in the heavyweight division, but I could see that times were changing and the whole scene as far as the higher weight class was concerned was swinging towards larger and larger wrestlers. My weight gradually built up to past the 20-stone mark and I decided against keeping it in check. Over a period of months, I levelled off at 23st and have stayed in that region ever since. However, with the extra weight, it called for a change of style, and I decided the time had come to make every pound and every bit of bulk count. This was how the belly-butt and Big Daddy image was born."

By 1966, Count Bartelli was becoming a TV regular, and the Commonwealth champion was de-masked by Kendo Nagasaki in front of the cameras. That year also saw the emergence of Lincoln's fighter Wayne Bridges, who went on to win a European title. In March, a few months before the competition was to begin, the football World Cup trophy was stolen during a public exhibition in Westminster Hall. In one of the most bizarre events in the history of sport, the trophy turned up seven days later. It was wrapped in newspaper in a hedge and found at the bottom of a garden in Upper Norwood, South London, by a mixed-breed collie named Pickles. As we know, the English team went on to lift the trophy four months later, famously beating Germany 4-2 in the final.

Afterwards, the dog was invited to a celebration banquet where, as a reward, he was allowed to lick his owner's bowl. The thief was never caught, and suspicion was placed upon Pickles (and his owner) for a while. The police didn't even get the chance to rough them up because Pickles sadly died, choking on his lead while out chasing a cat.

The summer of 1966 was sizzling, and songs like 'Sunny Afternoon' by The Kinks, and the Rolling Stones' hit 'Paint it Black' set the tone. The streets were hot and filling up with hippies turning on, tuning in, and dropping out. Near Woodstock, Bob Dylan was injured in a motorcycle accident, and in New York City ground-breaking work began at the site that would become the ill-fated World Trade Center. Back home in Halifax, the Victoria copperworks were damaged by fire, and in a freak turn of events flooding ruined the Halifax Show. Before his tragic death in 1967, there was one more moment of glory for Pickles, and he appeared alongside Eric Sykes and June Whitfield in the film *The Spy With the Cold Nose*.

In the world of wrestling Judo Mike Hamill (who later became "Kung-Fu" Eddie Hamill) turned professional, and Bert Assirati was still going at it hammer and tongs. He fought Australian Roy Heffernan in India, and within a few minutes, he had a bloodied nose. The Indians went mad when Heffernan tried to give it back to him. They didn't allow the spilling of blood, so the fight was stopped. Afterwards, Bert being his usual piss-taking self, hugged his opponent and said: "You're a very good boy, come fight in England", despite being only a few years away from pensionable age.

The year ended with the theft of paintings worth millions of pounds from an art gallery in Dulwich, London, on 31 December as everybody was out getting tanked up on Double Diamond and Babycham.

In January 1967, Mick McManus suffered his first defeat in front of the TV cameras and he was not a happy man. He refused to be on the same bill with the man who beat him (Peter Preston), and it was only when chance brought the two men together years later that they were even in the same room as one other.

In Manchester "Gentleman" Jimmy Lewis formed the Wrestlers' Union, and negotiated wages which still remained poor. All but the very top of the bill had to supplement their incomes to survive. If you were at the bottom of the card, you got six pounds, the supporting bout got eight, and top of the bill got a tenner. Each pound was hard earned and the way Max was with money didn't help. One night when they were fighting at the Eldorado in Leith, he started to call Sam Betts and the Barnsley lads "trouble-makers".

On the bill with Sam was Shirley and Karl Von Kramer, and after dropping the Leeds lads off at Leeds railway station to make their own ways home, Max paid them all their wages in a little brown envelope as usual before speeding off in the van. When the lads opened their pay packets they discovered that he had only paid them £2.50 each and they were absolutely livid.

Debuting in 1967 as Luke McMasters, Martin Ruane would go on to become Big Daddy's arch-nemesis Giant Haystacks, a true colossus of a man. When he was stood in the middle of the ring beneath the lights, his face twisted in mock anger beneath his beard, it really became apparent how much damage the guy could do if all 40-plus stone of him fell on you. He would be there glaring at Daddy, who would be stamping his feet and shaking his shoulders as the two men worked up the crowd. They were not the first to do this, but they were certainly two of the biggest. Other men have had greater wrestling contests, but few showed such showmanship and had a greater following, and they first clashed in a wrestler versus wrestler contest on 24 July 1975 in Digbeth.

"Haystacks comes from a family of giants and was being trained as a classically trained pianist before his fingers simply became too large for him to play properly. In wrestling he began throwing his weight about with a lot of success and it was not unnatural that somebody should have the idea of bringing Giant Haystacks and Big Daddy together as a tag team. They did – and it was hate at first sight. We just couldn't stand one another and this was a contest that

*was short-lived to say the least. We were together in
one bout at the Royal Albert Hall against Rex Strong
and Kendo Nagasaki in 1977, but the next occasion we
were in that famous ring was as opponents."*

The late 1960s was a time slightly lacking in direction for Shirley, and he even went back to life guarding in Blackpool during the summer. It can never be said that all his years as a wrestler were glorious, and that his rise from obscurity was not littered with failures and broken marriages as he searched for a bit of inner peace. Broken bones, absent children, and figuring out how to make ends meet was something he wasn't unfamiliar with either. The world was changing ever so quickly, and if you weren't fast enough you got left behind.

Brian once said that picking on one Crabtree meant the other two came running, but for a while, the brothers seemed to be going in different directions as Max's stature grew. It is just unfortunate that he treated so poorly some of the people he had working for him. There were always going to be chancers and piss-takers and nobody is suggesting it is all one-sided. Sometimes he didn't know where to stop, and he crossed the line with his own brothers too. Towards the end of Shirley's life, he was driving down the Queens Road in Halifax with his family when up on a billboard, he saw himself advertising a newly launched alcoholic drink. Apart from the fact he wasn't a drinker he knew nothing about the advert and when he rang Max up mad as hell, Max simply said: "Oh, I was about to tell you about that."

It was Norman Berry who once said wrestlers should be locked up in little pigeon coops on the Yorkshire Moors and only let out to fight, and Max adopted a similar philosophy. It was all about money, and many of those who weren't happy with Max felt Shirley was part of that problem. The truth is Shirley never changed as a person even when the brass did come rolling in. There were no airs and graces with him, he was happy with who he was and wasn't one to complain. He certainly came over as the least big-headed of the three and, for every person who bunches all three of the Crabtree brothers together and calls them arrogant, there is another who will defend Shirley.

Looking back at this with 40 years of hindsight, the lasting impression Max has left, despite how he breathed new life into the business, is that he was pretty ruthless. His methodology worked for a long while, but surely there would have been a way to do what he did with a bit of compassion for the lads that were taking the hammerings night after night. After all, he had once been in the same boat. When Shirley got to the top, he had waited so long that he had given up hope. He had to really push his rapidly depleting powers to the very limit to ensure that he stayed at the top, and he did this with a more kindly attitude. Max would promote rising yeast if he thought it would turn a penny, and the way he sometimes conducted his business has tarred all three brothers with the same brush. Shirley could be a pain in the arse, and Brian as egotistical as hell, but all three boys were quite different when it came down to it.

Chapter Eight
The Rise Of The Crabtrees

IN SEPTEMBER 1967, Shirley was asked to promote a fight between an Indian world champion called Dara Singh and the Pakistani champion Akram Gama. An expert at the forearm smash, Singh really put Indian wrestling on the map when he showed off his skills abroad, and was reported never to have been defeated in a wrestling ring. Real name Akram Pehlwan, Gama was a part of the famous Bholu Brothers tag team. He was also a very hard man that nobody would fight in the west until he offered £5,000 through promoter Orig Williams to anybody who could beat him. The money brought about a challenger, and he fought Anglo-French heavyweight champion Henry Perry for the world heavyweight title in London, and he beat him. This was of course sizable news at the time, and when a Bradford group of Pakistanis asked Shirley to promote a bout between the two great fighters he jumped at the chance.

These were the days when a shrewd entrepreneurial streak could earn you big bucks, and acting in good faith, Shirley hired the Keighley RLFC ground at Lawkholme Lane for the bout to take place. In the end, 3,000 fans turned up, and as soon as they shut the gates the Bradford group had it away on their toes with the takings. Billed as the "Pride of India", Singh failed to turn up as he was reported to be fighting in London on the same night. When this was announced the rival fans started to rip up the turf, and they started throwing it at each other and at the men in the ring, and of course Shirley had no money to give them a refund. He learned a valuable lesson that night as he looked out at the ensuing riot and ducked incoming projectiles.

Referee Jim Angus was not so lucky as when the old man got on the mic to appeal for calm he was hit on the bugle by a massive turf of mud and grass, and if the situation hadn't been so serious it would have been comical. Scuffling had started in the stands, and seats were broken before the ring was invaded and the police were eventually drafted in to disperse the crowd.

A problem Joint Promotions had at the time was that the owners were starting to lose interest as they thought about retirement, and they were looking to sell up. The business needed life breathed into it, and they chose Max to do the CPR. By the early 1970s the rot had really started to set in, and they promoted him to manage almost all of the territories. His inventiveness came to the fore, and his ability to be a match-maker and discover new faces helped to give things a lift as he raised the profile of championship matches. He began to reignite the interest of the fans as he swept through the whole operation like a dose of Viagra, and the business didn't wilt for a good 12 or 13 years.

As Dickie Davies took control, the whole of *World of Sport* began to be produced by London Weekend Television. One of the biggest fights of the year was from Trowell on FA Cup Final day when Mick McManus drew with Felix Miquet.

News of Jack Harris's death that year came as a shock to all three of the brothers. He was a popular man originally heralding from Yorkshire, before moving down south to Plymouth, and has been fondly described by many as a gentleman, and a very hard fighter.

The year ended with the band Led Zeppelin making their American debut in Denver a couple of days after Apollo 8's Christmas Eve orbit of the Moon. At Wembley, on 28 December, that man McManus was top of the bill again, and you would never have guessed he was the man in command of shows in the south.

With his short, dyed black hair and pointy sideburns he had made himself invincible, and there were no guidelines in place to say it wasn't allowed, so this made Max sit up and take note of all the different strings Mick was pulling.

Saying that, a great many people have a lot of time for Mick. Like Shirley, he achieved massive fame, and he didn't seem to change as a person unless you pissed him off. The year ended with him knocking out Peter Szakacs as the business limped on with a good amount of empty seats in many venues. And when I say limped on, the wrestling was still doing well in terms of TV ratings, and the promoters weren't exactly going hungry like many of their fighters would have done without a second job.

Saturday afternoons regularly attracted audiences of eight million-plus, and the Wednesday night bouts usually topped the six-million mark, which was good. The problem was that people were less inclined to come out and brave the British weather when they could watch it in the comfort of their own homes on the old goggle-box. If you had the money, you could go and buy yourself a colour TV as the BBC had started its colour broadcasts in 1967 and the nation gradually changed from black and white. A licence for your new colour set cost a bit though, as in January 1968 you could get a combined licence for a black and white TV and a radio for a pound and five shillings. It was a fiver for a colour TV licence such was its luxury, a complete rip-off comparable to the introduction of other state-of-the-art technologies such as video recorders, Sky television, HD, and the George Foreman Grill.

The 1960s ended with martial law being declared in Madrid, Richard Nixon elected President of the USA, and Mark Rocco making his professional wrestling debut. Although mainly promoting now, Max was still wrestling in 1968, but neither of the brothers were breaking their backs in the ring, and Shirley figured his best days were behind him. He did a variety of different jobs to make ends meet at that point as he watched with pride his brother establish himself in the business.

It was difficult with Max's wife Beryl at times; there must have been the nagging question in Shirley's mind of why the two women had run away to Paris. Whether he did what his mum did when his dad left and blocked it out, or if he simply didn't care, it does look like he never really asked. And if he did have a chat when Max brought her back from Paris he never shared those secrets with anyone other than his brothers.

Going home to an empty house night after night would have most certainly been the cause of a lot of pain and suffering for Shirley. What is known is that the relationship the wives had formed with Monsieurs Gessat and Manneveau did not last. Beryl was gradually accepted back into the family circle, but there was still no reconciliation for Shirley and Sally and there never would be. She would eventually settle in Newport in Wales with Shirley's children Lionel and Catherine, who would take on the surname of Sally's new husband.

At the death knell of the decade, the bosses at Joint were casting an eye over a couple of new fighters. Pat Curry caught the eye of some of the bigger promoters and, on signing for Joint, many people believe he didn't receive the backing he should have been guaranteed, and one of the high-profile matches he was involved in was in October 1970, when he was knocked out by Kendo Nagasaki. Johnny Kincaid was another who joined the ranks at this time after dying his hair blonde, and Ray Robinson came and worked for Max after starting out with Cyril Knowles.

At the time, Shirley was wrestling independently as The Battling Guardsman, in recognition of the time he had spent in the Coldstream Guards. It was a great gimmick, and he came into ring in all the gear; Busby, medals, the lot. In his publicity photos we see him posing beside a cannon, with his hands upon his hips looking at the sky like he was preparing for the Battle of Britain. With that Busby, the photos show a rather patriotic image which went down well with the crowds, and he later returned to it with Big Daddy. In the late 1970s the Sex Pistols were taking the piss out of the monarchy and the establishment with their song 'God

Save the Queen'. By then Shirley had successfully crossed the patriotic gimmick, with a leotard, a codpiece, and a Union Jack, and created a John Bull-like character for the crowd to absorb.

So OK, Big Daddy was never going to change the world, or blind you with the greatest wrestling you would ever see, and he would not have got a look-in if he had been a WWF wrestler, but that was not what he was about. There was something Churchillian about him, without the cigar and the backwards two-fingered salute. The Daddy character was unique to its time period, and he gave everyone a good laugh whoever they were.

How many times it has been said he hated kids, and sometimes he probably cringed at the thought of signing autographs. Imagine being physically and mentally drained with a five-hour drive back home. You would want to be gone as soon as you had stepped out of the ring. Despite the image of the Daddy superhero, Shirley was only human, and he did what he could and put so many smiles on so many people's faces he would certainly have got something from all of that on a good day. It wasn't always for the cameras as some have also suggested, it really didn't matter what he did, his presence was enough to make people happy.

Ray Robinson recalls how he could get up on the mic and talk, and he would have the complete attention of kids, grandparents, and parents so much that they would forget about the wrestling.

> "I had been wrestling as 'Shirley Crabtree', the Blonde Adonis, and as Mr Universe (before the Battling Guardsman). I was well muscled in those days and only weighed about 15st, but I realised that in wrestling, as in boxing, the real interest is in the heavyweights… It became obvious to me that the British heavyweight division was crying out for a figure who, whilst flamboyant, was someone the fans of all ages could identify with, and I set about making Big Daddy just that person. The response was fantastic and whilst my earlier career had not been without success, it was

*nothing to the almost overnight impact of Big Daddy.
I have always been able to look after myself in the ring
and have enjoyed my fair share of support from the
fans, but what started to happen at tournaments was
little short of incredible."*

The 1970s started with an earthquake in Yunnan, China, which killed over 15,000 people. A few days later Diana Ross left the Supremes after a farewell concert at the Frontier Hotel in Las Vegas. At the end of January, Mick Jagger was caught with a stash of cannabis on him and was fined £200, and the Half Crown coin ceased to be legal tender. Events were starting to take shape, and they would soon bring together both Martin Ruane and Shirley Crabtree.

In the early 1970s, Martin began working for wrestling enterprises as Haystacks Calhoun, after the US wrestler William Calhoune. He soon changed his name to Giant Haystacks, and with the popularity of the super-heavyweight division increasing, Joint were quick to get him on their books, as they did with Shirley. In an attempt to bolster attendances there were some big-name fights in early 1970, but most of them were televised, which sort of defeated the object. The bosses at Joint were treading a fine line at the time; they had to put on the best shows with the biggest names for the TV, but they had to leave something in the pot for the live shows and make it worthwhile coming out and spending money, so there was a lot of pressure to keep things fresh.

There were other fantastic promotions out there, but somehow they managed to fend off the opposition. If there had not been a change of management during this time, and a reignition of enthusiasm, the Joint cartel would have fallen flat on its face, so Max getting more involved was a good move. The most reliable fighters were getting regular work, filling up the bill for the stars who could of course be difficult. When Max gained control it felt like the whole business had been shocked back to life, and the razzmatazz he created worked. However, it had more the feel of a seaside resort show, with hooded men covered in tinsel, glitter, and tinfoil, than a hghi-profile, no-expense-spared, WWF performance. Ten, five-minutes rounds of average technical wrestling (without the theatrics) is about as enjoyable as root-canal treatment, so the high jinks and tomfoolery put into the routines was what beefed up the performance, and it was more exciting than custard pies and clowns.

The jewel in the crown of British seaside resorts is the Blackpool Pleasure Beach, and it is a place ingrained in many people's childhood memories; be it for the rollercoasters and sticks of rock, or the vodka jellies in The Laughing Donkey and then the bunk-up under the pier before the last tram home. Everybody loves Blackpool for their own reason.

The Pleasure Beach itself was founded in 1896 by a chap called Mr Bean, and expanded by a Mr Outhwaite in 1903 to recreate the famous Coney Island in America. They wanted to make adults feel like children, and they certainly were successful with all the lovely attractions. A gutful of dodgy cockles, and half-a-dozen pickled onions and the only bit of your childhood you would have wanted back was the nappies. Many came close to Roger Bannister's record, wearing just espadrilles or flip-flops, hurtling towards the public conveniences like there was no tomorrow. Failure was not an option as you would have to claw the tuppence out of the secret pocket of your swimwear, get it in the slot, and debunk like a jack-in-the-box in reverse if you were going to avoid the ultimate embarrassment.

Many a man would be straight in the sea after a portion of such sea front delicacies had entered a stomach already boasting six pints of stout and last night's kebab. A spot of swimming in the rain and borderline hypothermia would be the next turn of events, right towards the point of hallucination. With the Lancastrian tones of George Formby shouting "he-he mother, turned out nice again!" ringing in your head, and a distorted fairground organ somewhere off in the distance striking up "we're going to hang out the washing on the Siegfried line", the walk of shame would begin. Amused grannies sat in wheelchairs licking cornets, eight-year-old boys jamming drachmas into the fortune-telling machine, would turn to watch the John Wayne shuffle up the beach, which was dramatic enough to stop the Mods and Rockers rowing.

All of the greats played Blackpool, be it one of its ballrooms, the pier, the Winter Gardens, or under the Tower. From AC/DC to Wurlitzer Wizard Howard Finch, Peter Kaye and Sid Lowe, everyone did a turn at Blackpool, and the wrestlers were no different. The North Pier was where it all happened; and Shirley fought there many times during the course of his career.

The first major attraction to open at the Pleasure Beach was the Hiram Maxim Captive Flying Machine in 1904, and after that they added water rides, a Noah's Ark, a big dipper, and dodgems. In the 1920s a casino was opened, and on a bit of reclaimed land they expanded operations with rollercoasters and, of course, the famous illuminations. When they started out they were lit by gas, and first went electric on Princess Parade in May 1912 to mark the first royal visit to the town.

When you think of Blackpool, you can almost imagine Kenneth Williams, Barbara Windsor, Sid James and Hattie Jacques strolling along the seafront wearing those bloody kiss-me-quick hats and eating candy floss. Blackpool is the ancestral home of the "British holiday", in a time before budget airline flights to Majorca, and wine-tasting breaks to Champagne via EuroStar.

To accommodate the influx of seasonal visitors, hotels and guesthouses started to spring up, and after a while Shirley found a nice friendly little place to stay, although the food was only worth eating if the owner Eunice Wright wasn't cooking. When they met, Eunice was married with four children, but they struck up quite a friendship as Shirley spent more and more time in the town.

He eventually moved to Blackpool and was only wrestling occasionally, having spent the 1960s working for Max, Jack Taylor, Cyril Knowles, Paul Lincoln, and then the Bholu Brothers during their tour of Britain in 1967. The following year, he teamed up with his brother Max once again, and formed his own carnival sideshow which he ran out of Blackpool. At the time, the Crabtrees were running wrestling shows from many of the nightclubs and dance halls in the town, and it is this operation which really made people sit up and take notice of what they were doing.

If Shirley didn't want any hassle, he simply did his White Angel gimmick in a mask, but it is here that Max's organisational skills in particular got him noticed. That and the fact he wouldn't take any messing, but the bosses really were impressed by the way he went about their business. With Max on board, he wanted both of his brothers involved, especially Shirley, who had been the main motivator and driving force behind many of his decisions.

In the early 1970s, people like Black Sabbath and Jimmy Hendrix played in and around the Blackpool area; and Pink Floyd went on the piss with a Welsh band called Amen Corner and had all their stuff stolen overnight.

There was money to be made if you were in the entertainment game, and the Crabtrees saw a revival of their fortunes. Something was troubling Shirley around this time, and if he had been able to sort it out the other guy would have surely ended up in the hospital.

He had become romantically involved with Eunice Wright, who was a former ballroom dancer. Always the life and soul of the party she was prone to turn on people if she'd had a few drinks, but she wasn't really introduced to alcohol until she became familiar with Max's wife Beryl, who would often come down from the farm armed with drink when the men were away.

When Shirley first met Eunice, she was very much the victim of alcoholism herself. She was married to a man called Arthur Wright, and they had four children of their own. Arthur was a whiskey drinker, and he thought it was fun to get tanked up and belt Eunice. How much she told Shirley about the situation back then is unknown, but she must have kept quite a bit of it from him because he certainly wouldn't have stood for it.

The fact is there were children involved; the youngest was Jane, and it was her, more than any of the others, who formed a lasting bond with Shirley. She became the daughter he had once lost, and their endearing relationship lasted until he took his final breath. In fact, he took on all four children once Arthur was gone, and lived the rest of his life being blamed by the two eldest daughters (Linda and Carole) for the break-up of their family, which just wasn't true. They effectively divorced their mother once they were old enough to leave home, and after putting themselves in care, they eventually ran off and married a couple of Teddy Boys and made their own lives.

There was also Paul, Jane's older brother, and with these two children they became a family. Jane was too young to remember what had gone on in the family home before Shirley arrived on the scene, but it had not been pleasant, and falling in love with Shirley gave Eunice the strength she needed to finally leave her wife-beating husband. She took a crazy last-minute trip to Vienna with Shirley (who was wrestling over there once again) and it was during this time that they really fell for each other, and they had such a good laugh.

The biggest problem they faced was that they were skint, and they knew that when they eventually checked out of the hotel that they were going to have problems, but they just did not have the money. It wasn't a dignified exit for the former British and European champion but it was necessary. If they had been caught the consequences would have been grave, but they really didn't have the cash if they wanted to eat.

It is not unknown for people to leave hotels with the dressing-gowns and towels; some even take the tea and coffee, soap and shampoo. Others have had the TV away, and a few have left the hotel via the window, and that is exactly what Shirley and Eunice had to do. It is hard to imagine a man the size of Shirley shimmying down the drain pipe and avoiding settling the bill, and when his new woman came tumbling into his arms straight after they were laughing so much they were very lucky they didn't get caught.

British and European Champion Shirley Crabtree in 1960. Seen here with brothers Max (second left) and Brian (second right).

Shirley loved nothing more than walking the Dales, and there was usually a dog or two in tow.

Bert Assirati.

Shirley in the 1960s.

Ready for action: Shirley, Brian, and Max.

As the Battling Guardsman. Shirley joined the guards for his national service in the fifties, and used the busby as a gimmick. He tapped into the audience's sense of patriotism, and returned to it once again as Daddy.

Siddal RLFC 1947/48. Shirley towers above everyone else in the back row.

Not topping the bill yet, but soon.

A 16-stone training dummy which Shirley used in his gym every day to maintain his strength.

A sullen moment, but fame and fortune was just around the corner.

Malcolm "King Kong" Kirk, who was accidentally killed in the ring by Shirley in August 1987.

The man – the legend.

Daddy versus John Quinn at Wembley.

Tony "Banger" Walsh who fought Daddy over 700 times without a single victory.

Commentator Kent Walton.

Other big names back in the day. Mick McManus versus Jackie Pallo.

Enjoying a rare moment of peace and quiet. Shirley loved to read, and was as comfortable with a book by Keats or Oscar Wilde, as he was with the paper.

There goes another sunbed!

With youngest daughter Jane – they were the best of friends.

Signing autographs for friends, sometimes for hours after the show.

Feel the power – Bill Pearl does!

British Icon showing his support during the Falklands War.

From the photoshoot for the 1983 Big Daddy annual.

The evolution of Shirley's swimming pools.

With third wife Eunice during happier moments.

Daddy's girl Jane.

On Blackpool Pier reliving his life-guarding days.

Striking another patriotic pose.

Arch enemy Giant Haystacks aka Martin Ruane.

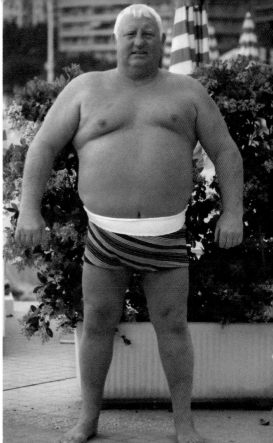

Shirley once made the Guinness Book of Records because of the size of his shoulders. Despite the weight he put on as Daddy he still had the build of a bodybuilder at the peak of his fame.

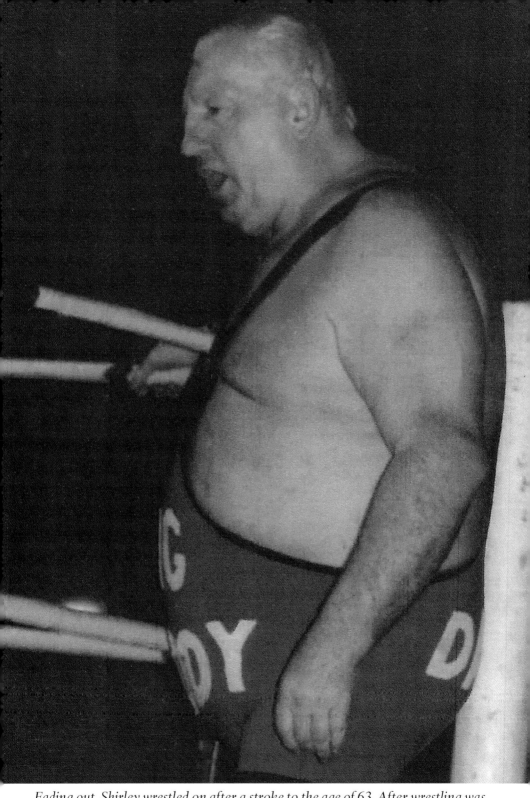

Fading out. Shirley wrestled on after a stroke to the age of 63. After wrestling was cancelled from the TV scheduling only the name of Big Daddy on the bill would guarantee seats being sold.

Picking up the suitcases they had thrown out into the garden, they made off into the night like Bonnie and Clyde.

For a while, there was that element of notoriety in their relationship. When you're starving hungry or freezing cold you sometimes have to do what you have to do. There was one instance when Shirley had helped himself in a motorway café near Birmingham and actually got caught by the manager and was asked to leave straight away.

Before leaving Britain, Eunice had left the children with her estranged husband which was probably a bit of a reckless thing to do but he was their father. After she left, Arthur took the kids to their grandparents in St Helens, saying he had some errands to attend to, and he never returned. It was irresponsible of Eunice to leave her children like she did and her two eldest daughters blamed Shirley for splitting up the family despite the way their father had behaved. In their anger towards their mother and her new man, they were, in fact, blinkered from the truth, and in recent years Jane has been able to put across the other side of the story. What is a shame is that they couldn't have learned more about the truth while Shirley was still alive, but they simply weren't aware that their father had abandoned them.

The summer of 1972 was all about Watergate and on 17 June five White House operatives were arrested for breaking into the offices of the Democratic National Committee in Washington and they had it away on their toes with money that they put into a slush fund. When it was discovered that the recording systems in the White House had taped conversations that implicated the President, it was curtains for Richard Nixon. In a parting gesture, he announced that no new draftees would be going out to Vietnam before his resignation in 1974.

Only 270 miles away from Munich and the Olympics taking place in five weeks' time, Vienna was a hive of activity when Shirley returned with Eunice in June 1972. Then there was the massacre of the Israeli Olympic team by the Palestinian group Black September, and this overshadowed the Games. There was, however, Greco-Roman and freestyle wrestling during the Games, and it was the Soviet Union who came away with nine gold medals.

The records show that Shirley was involved in three fights against Billy White Wolfe in Vienna that summer. White was really an Iraqi called Adnan Al-Kaissie. The year before he fought Shirley, he defeated Andre the Giant at the Al-Shaab Stadium, but the most worrying thing about the man was the fact that he was mates with Saddam Hussein.

On returning to England, Shirley fought Gargantua, Leon Arras, Tug Holton, and Steve Haggarty for Joint Promotions towards the end of the year. On Boxing Day, he was appearing as the international star Battling Guardsman, and he was up against Ron Parkes in Bridlington.

Chapter Nine

As Seen On TV

IN MAY 1971, the spacecraft Mariner 8 failed to launch. Unlike Mariner 8, the Rolling Stones did the complete opposite. Their single 'Brown Sugar/Bitch/Let It Rock' rose upwards at terrific speed until it was almost at the top of the UK top 40 singles chart.

At this period in his life, Shirley was appearing as himself, The Guardsman, The Mighty Guardsman, and a few other names. Kendo Nagasaki was doing his first television around this time, and now Shirley was back in with Joint he was hoping it wouldn't be long until it was his turn in front of the cameras.

Kendo ended up beating Wayne Bridges on the night of his TV debut, and this was the beginning of a love-hate televised relationship between the villainous Kendo and the viewer. Sometimes controversial, he was always good value for money, and he stayed on our screens for over 15 years. In July, during a sensational TV contest against Billy Howes, his mask came off in the heat of battle and caused all-round confusion. Howe was pounding him in the head and dragging the tight-fitting garment up towards his eyes when the straps came loose. Forgetting the fight, Howe just wanted to de-mask him, so Kendo left the ring and covered his face.

By December he had some support. His manager Gorgeous George made his debut in Dumfries and he went with Kendo on his tour of Canada and North America in 1972, and he was certainly played a big part in Kendo's success with his outrageously camp performances. Other stars were emerging at this point in time; Eddie Hamill (The Amazing Kung-Fu) started out fighting in a mask as Judo Ed Hamill, and he enthralled the crowd with his speed and agility. "Mucky" Mal Kirk was also at the peak of his powers in 1971, and he beat Mike Marino at the Royal Albert Hall in a tournament win. Years later, Shirley and Mal would face each other in the ring in a tag contest. They had done this many times before but this would be the last, and tragically Kirk's final seconds of life would stay in Shirley's mind for the rest of his days.

Although he could never be described as a glam rocker, Shirley's comeback saw him don all manner of glittery costumes and there is still film floating around of him fighting in a green leotard in 1972. At this point in time, although he had put on a bit of weight, he was quite muscular, and a couple of stone shy of the weight he would achieve as Big Daddy.

Already he was looking towards reinventing himself as a character people could relate to, and with Eunice making his costumes they gradually got better. When he started out they were dreadful, and looked like they were made out of old sets of curtains and cushions, which of course, they were. There was even a cream leotard with a mint Paisley design which had once been a well-known curtain for one of the leading high-street retailers. Very much on the comeback trail, 42-year-old Shirley did OK in Vienna despite the financial hardship. When he returned to Britain with Eunice, they managed to get some money together, so they went and got the children from Eunice's parents and moved to Leeds. For Jane, living above a sweet shop was brilliant, and they were only 60 miles away from St Helens. They spent a good deal of time with their grandparents while Eunice followed Shirley wrestling all around the country.

It was then that the two eldest girls put themselves into care, as things were up in the air a lot of the time, and there wasn't a lot of stability. Shirley became the steadying influence, and when he wasn't wrestling, he and his new family would spend their time going on day trips, and later, when he had made his money, foreign holidays. Despite all the hardship, his stepdaughter Jane recalls these times with great fondness. These were the golden years of her life with the man who became a brilliant father to her. Later, when he was famous, there was even more demand upon his time and energy, but no matter what time he arrived home in the morning he would always come up and tuck her into bed with a kiss on the cheek, a bag of sweets, or a dodgy watch he'd bought off one of the wrestlers or spivs.

> *"My parents always told me they had decided to christen me Shirley after a character in one of the Bronte novels, and I also took to literature and got the idea of Big Daddy from a character from the man in the Tennessee Williams book Cat on a Hot Tin Roof. At first, it was 'Big Daddy' Crabtree that appeared on the posters but in a short time the surname was dropped and Big Daddy really caught on… Eunice is a genius with a needle and cotton, and I didn't take her seriously when she suggested I should go for a more colourful image. At first, I wasn't too keen, and then she produced such bright and attractive capes and gowns that I was won over, and I have been wearing them ever since."*

Shirley's comeback for Joint Promotions in 1972 was at first for Norman Morrell and Ted Beresford fighting as a super-heavyweight and not for Max as is the popular belief. On 2 September he shocked TV fans by knocking out Pat Curry in his TV debut in Staffordshire. It was his first time in front of the cameras and he entered the ring in the Guardsman's costume, and he towered over his opponent. During the first round, Curry was thrown across the ring three times before trying to get Shirley into a headlock. His forearm smashes weren't even felt by the big man and he was thrown out of the ring in the second round and landed badly. The crowd booed and stamped as Shirley issued a challenge to any wrestler in the world and thus the shenanigans began.

He was next in front of the cameras at the end of the month and won again by knockout. This time it was at the expense of Pete Roberts as promoters booked Shirley on a winning run. It wasn't until the mid-1970s that Max became the northern area booker and when Shirley started to work for him that winning run was extended indefinitely.

It was Jack Dale and Les Martin who first took Max on board because he had been doing so well in Scotland, although his shows were not known for their glitz, and they sometimes lacked finesse. Before the end of the year, Shirley had beaten Steve Haggarty, Leon Arras, and Tug Holton, before the rematch against Pete Curry in Darlington in November ended in a no contest. A further two victories against Terry Rudge at Belle Vue, and Dr Death, put Shirley right up at the top, and he was finally beaten by Kendo Nagasaki in Winsford in January 1973. Billed as the "immovable object" meeting the "irresistible force", in an incredible feat of strength Kendo lifted Shirley on to his shoulders and calmly walked to the corner where he finished the bout with an amazing "Kamikaze Crash".

The tabloids were full of wrestling exposé in 1972, as the *News of the World* published dressing room conversations between Mike Marino and Albert Wall on how the fight was going to go. It caused a bit of a stir and then sank without a trace until the mid-1980s, but the truth is you had to have been pretty special if you genuinely believed the wrestling was totally legit. Perhaps you were a 40-year-old chap still living with mum and subscribing to the *Eagle* comic, or you weren't allowed out after dark because of the voices, and while most fights maintained a high level of credibility it is true to say that some were just crap.

The level of punishment these fighters supposedly dished out would have left any man in a coma, or a semi-vegetative state, not charging back at their opponent at full speed. Accidents did happen in the ring, our man Bert Assirati actually broke a man's back in Germany, so things didn't always go to plan. There is recorded testimony of Max and many others saying none of his fights were rigged but what else could they have said? It was generally agreed that one fighter would let the other do his special moves on him, and then there would be a role-reversal.

While the outcome of the fight was usually known, if the crowd suddenly took to a wrestler booked to lose the result could change. Max would be stood in the wings watching the action like a football manager, ready to make a change if the crowd went flat. This was a private area for wrestlers, and wrestling people, and although the Crabtree kids were allowed to sit ringside and watch, they were never allowed anywhere nearer. They understood their father when he was at home, and they understood him when he was at work. The apron could be a pretty harrowing place and if the crowd reaction was negative and the fight had gone flat Max might ask one of the fighters to get out a Stanley knife and cut themselves for which they would receive an extra fiver in their wages.

The wrestling moved from a Wednesday to a Tuesday evening in 1972, just as an 18-year-old called Marty Jones was emerging. At the time technical wrestling was giving way to more and more showmanship and gimmicks. Shirley himself was past his fighting best, and his style was slower, so he began to rely more heavily on his size and strength, and later certain wrestlers were asked to slow things down to accommodate. Shirley could still take a knock, and if these had been true contests his power and strength would have meant he could have gone toe-to-toe with most.

Marty was a skilled heavyweight who could hold his own with many of the top professionals, but he was unfortunate enough to arrive upon the scene when a unique gimmick heightened reputations. Trained by Billy Roberts, he became a brilliant villain and knew how to work the crowd. His legendary feuds with fighters such as Fit Finlay usually ended in blood, and he became the world mid-heavyweight champion after Mike Marino died in

1982. Of course, flair and technical ability were always desired in any wrestler, but this new type of showmanship wrestling with its carnival technique created superheroes in the ring. What was expected from wrestlers became more and more fantastical, and moved further away from what can be done in real life, and it is here that our comic-book hero analogy becomes relevant.

By blurring the lines between reality and fiction so well, professional wrestling in Britain set itself up for a fall long-term, and when the Crabtrees' empire did finally collapse it was because it could not compete with what was coming in from America. Besides this, many of the other top acts in Britain were past their fighting prime, but as we mentioned earlier, some of the up-and-coming youngsters did find success in America.

Even Martin Ruane got a chance over there in 1996 despite being 50 years old. Fighting as Loch Ness rather than Haystacks, he feuded with Hulk Hogan before he was diagnosed with the cancer which ended his life in late 1998.

Shirley's defeat against Kendo in January 1973 was only a momentary blip. As the super-tug boat *Statesman* was sent out to protect British fishing vessels from Icelandic ships during the cod war, all 24st of Shirley was sent crashing into the ring against Count Bartelli in Hanley a few days later for another flabbergasting win. The crowd went batty once again when he beat him again in Halifax a couple of weeks later, and he was finally bitten by the man with the shiny pants and the vampire gimmick the very next night in Nantwich.

Work was starting to come in regularly now, and of course it helped being employed by old friends and having a brother who wielded so much power within the organisation. By February 1973, Shirley was doing three or four shows a week, so he bought an A35 van and put a bed in the back just in case he had to doss down for the night in some layby. It also meant that Jane could come to the wrestling with her dad, and she would sleep in the back while Shirley drove them home after she had seen him fight and had a supper of fish and chips and fizzy pop. She witnessed so many great nights before Shirley's meteoric rise to the top of the profession, but being so young she remembers the electric atmosphere more than the wrestling.

They did some miles in that van with its 1,000cc engine, but it was a great way for a young girl to see the country, rather than being stuck at home in front of the TV. When they eventually moved from Leeds to Millbank, Eunice took it upon herself to paint the van, which she did with a pot of blue paint and a brush. She did a shocking job, and there were streaks and brush strokes all over the place. All Shirley would have needed was a "ban the bomb" symbol and some flowers painted on the bonnet and he could have gone off and joined a hippy commune.

By the end of 1972, Atari had released the arcade version of Pong, and the last executions by guillotine had taken place in Paris. On Boxing Day, there was televised wrestling and Eddie Capelli beat Clive Myers in Lewisham. Paul McCartney and Wings had the Christmas number one with their poignant hit 'Mull of Kintyre' reflecting the festive mood of the nation. In America, President Harry H. Truman died, and still the country was wrapped up in Vietnam and Watergate.

Back home in Yorkshire Max, Brian and their families had bought a farm in Sowerby Bridge which Brian had renovated and they set up their homes in separate cottages. Shirley would later follow them to the nearby village of Millbank, but for the time being he stayed in Leeds because it was a good middle ground for everything they had going on in Blackpool and Halifax. The idea to first move from Leeds arose purely through convenience. As the business was building up, and Shirley was getting ever more popular, it just seemed like the right thing to do.

The Crabtree brothers were working pretty closely together once again, and it felt like the old days when they were finding their feet in the clubs as well as in the ring. The difference now was that they were all a bit older and they all had families, so there was no big-risk taking, everything they did had to be more calculated to make the most out of a particular situation. They were travelling together to various shows in the beginning, although this became less frequent when Big Daddy emerged. Having to travel to Leeds every night to pick up Shirley before they set off to Scotland, or Newcastle, was a royal pain in the arse.

It was then that Shirley moved the family into a renovated weaver's cottage in Millbank, and it was just far enough away from the farm so that his brothers and their families wouldn't come knocking on the door every five minutes and Shirley could have a bit of peace and quiet. Working with his brothers was enough, and although they had many great social occasions, it was the real fortitude of the village with its granite buildings that Shirley loved. On a typical day off, after he had trained and eaten, he would love nothing more than looking out of the window at the Dales as he listened to a bit of Roy Orbison or Dire Straits and skimmed through the paper. He could be quite quiet and introspective if he was winding down after a busy week. On other occasions, he could be reciting poetry or prose much to the amusement of the family before they took the dogs for a walk prior to Eunice burning the Sunday lunch.

There was no hassle in the village from the locals, even when Shirley became a star. If you saw a neighbour or school teacher down at the shops there would be a cheery hello but nothing else. It was only when Shirley ventured out into the big wide world that he got asked for autographs, but of course, it was all part of being a famous personality who people recognised instantly.

> *"Most folk are kind and don't want nothing but a signature and a little bit of chit-chat. By and large they are lovely people who say complimentary things, they have their two minutes, and they are on their way. Occasionally, you get a wise guy, someone who wants to take the mickey, but you just have to laugh them off. Big Daddy is a character of myth and fantasy for all those kids out there, like Santa Claus or the Pied Piper. Of course, they want to see me beating baddies in the ring*

but what they don't want to see are pictures of me having
a barney in the street on the front pages of the papers."

The safeness of the village was another big draw for Shirley, who would be away from home quite a bit so he didn't want the family stuck in the middle of Leeds where they didn't really know anybody. Millbank was a sleepy little place where everybody knew each other and nobody batted an eyelid to any of the Crabtree clan as they went about their business. It was an idyllic childhood for the children of the village, and their parents didn't need to know where they were when they were out playing because they knew they were safe. They could take themselves off to play in the fields or the woods and only come home when it started to get dark, or they heard the jingling bell of the ice cream van, or the theme tune to *Top of the Pops.*

People respected Shirley's privacy when he became popular, and he appreciated that. He wouldn't hesitate to exchange small talk with his neighbours, whether it was about the wrestling or not, and if it was the birthday of one of the local children or something was happening in the school he was more than happy to make an appearance and sign photos, or to give out a couple of free tickets.

It seemed to be those from outside who wanted to touch the famous television personality, and when somebody becomes famous the glare of the media spotlight and diminishing privacy and personal space can become a tremendous burden.

It is hard to pinpoint what it actually was that made Big Daddy a national icon, as there wasn't one particular skill that Shirley was an absolute expert in. Whenever he turned up, it would be fun, and the more popular he became the greater the expectation there was for him to have a public voice. He certainly had his fair share of nerves in front of the camera when he was being interviewed or making an appearance in the studio, and this sort of TV was totally different to wrestling in front of the cameras. And as much as people moan about how crap the money and conditions were, the truth is they would have done it all for nothing if there was the chance to be on TV.

Many members of the Crabtree family would settle in and around Millbank and Sowerby Bridge, but back in the day the kids would enjoy going up to the farm to ride uncle Brian's horses. Shirley and Jane would often go out and walk the dogs, ending up at the farm for a cup of tea. The men would then go off into the back room to talk business, while the kids rode the horses over the fields.

During the course of Shirley's life there would be as many ups and downs as there were in the Dales, but as Jane grew up she had some memorable family times with both of her parents. Shirley was happy to let Eunice deal largely with the finances and run the house, and she made sure his tea was always on the table. During those early days when he was getting ever more popular, grandparents Alf and Emily's house in St Helens was very much a second home for the children. There were two types of normality; there was at home with mum and dad, and staying with nan and granddad when they were away wrestling. Later gran would stay at the house when granddad Alf died, and Shirley got on really well with the both of them.

Jane and her gran would make Eccles cakes and egg custards which were his favourite. He also taught Jane how to tie her shoe laces by standing her in his great big boots and helping her tie the knots. They would usually end up on the floor rolling about with laughter, and for Shirley, it was the simplicity of family life in the village which gave him the vital release he needed, although he only ever had a couple of days off a week. Going to all the different cities and towns he had to go to, and all the miles in between was pretty hectic, so coming home would have been a complete switch-off for him. It would also have been where he was allowed to be Shirley Crabtree for a time, rather than his alter ego.

"Since Big Daddy became a household name in Britain and a good bit further afield, I have been

busier fulfilling engagements than at any other time in my life. And as with all wrestlers, the more bouts that are undertaken the greater the travelling involved and I have certainly done my share in the last two years…

As you grow older there is a natural tendency to want to slow things down more and there wasn't any possibility of doing so whilst Big Daddy was the name on the top of the bill selling the seats. It is the time you're allowed to just sit still, with no one to bother you and your family around you that you learn to appreciate."

On the corner of their property was a hairdressing salon and when it was vacated Shirley took on the lease and turned it into a gym. It wasn't massive, but it was big enough for him, and he was very religious about his training regimes even when he was in his later fighting years.

It is easy to see Big Daddy in a negative light as an athlete because of the weight he was carrying and his stamina later on but he still had to train if he wanted to continue as a professional wrestler or else you would get hurt. To get into the gym you had to go up a flight of stairs, and when you were sat next door in the house watching TV if Shirley was training and was using the punchbag the whole wall would shake, and it would feel like the place was going to fall down.

Sometimes Jane would wake up at the noise of her dad's car pulling up late at night or in the early hours. She would hear the key go in the lock, and after he had come up and tucked her in, he would be downstairs to polish his boots before he had his supper. It didn't matter what time he came home; he would always polish his boots, which is something he picked up from his days in the Coldstream Guards. There would be a quick prayer before he looked in the oven to see what Eunice had burned for his supper, and then he would be off to bed ready for the journey the following afternoon.

Chapter Ten

Enter Big Daddy

THE SWEET'S hit 'Block Buster' was the sound everyone was getting down to in their flares and platforms back in 1973. It was a truly hideous time to be a fashion icon and was a completely different look to that of the 1960s. With the emergence of the Beatles and the Stones, there was the short-back-and-sides, the mop-top, and the quiff, and some of the mods and rockers were putting razors in their collars. When Timothy Leary told everybody to turn on, tune in, and drop out, that's exactly what many did, much to the dismay of the establishment who branded them "the great unwashed". People were going on the road like Kerouac, or hanging out with the hippies and living in communes, or going between festivals, fairs, and other places of significance. They did have a tendency to chuck up a bit with their incense, body odour, and marijuana, but they were earthy souls and bathing was for wimps.

There was also another category of lofty hairstyles doing the rounds at this time as in the new decade there was a class of pop stars sporting big styles and really leading the way. With frizz reaching up into the sky like tributes to God himself, people like Michael Jackson, Leo Sayer, Minnie Riperton and Brian May were way out in front. Not only was the hair big, the sideburns sometimes took over the face, or got plaited in with protruding ear-hair.

Thin Lizzy's song 'Whiskey In The Jar' followed 'Block Buster' as one of the big hits at the time, and suddenly Phil Lynott was the man of the moment, but his mutton chops weren't in the same league as Noddy Holder's.

If you looked down the average street in Britain back then your view would have been blocked by a sea of endless bouffants; but Shirley always kept what was left of his hair cropped right back. Only Telly Savalas felt left out, but his slap-headed nature was soon compensated and his cop show *Kojak* became one of the most popular TV series of all time. The first episode aired in the States in 1973, and Telly would have made a good ring villain if he had ever fancied it – all of this without a single hair on his head.

Glam rock was also taking over with its glittery wide-awake style, and there were wrestlers who used both of these looks in their gimmicks. Haystacks was partial to the unkempt just stepped out of the bushes after thieving from your bins type of look, and at the time people like Marc Bolan and David Bowie were right up there with him although there barnets were a little more kempt. Wrestlers such as Adrian Street and Bobby Barnes capitalised on the early 1970s style, and they came up with their own camp-glam look when they started tagging as The Hells Angels.

None of these fashions affected Shirley of course, but there was a period of transition for him until Big Daddy came along. Up until then he had wrestled with and without gimmicks, and the problem with having an alter ego was that it had to prove itself. Some didn't work out, while others had some success. As the 1970s wore on all manner of weird and wonderful characters began to emerge as Shirley recalled:

> "Looking back at it now it was a strange time for me the middle of the 1970s. I was still pretty much unknown for the first half of the decade, but then my life changed overnight, and people started to notice me when I was out and about. This was of course

because of the television, but as my fame increased I became more private and guarded about my personal time and space. How one minute you can walk down a street without anybody hardly ever noticing you, and then the next everybody wants to shake your hand is quite remarkable and illustrates the power of the media. Although I've always been confident in myself and my abilities I would say appearing on television was sometimes overwhelming. When you're wrestling, you never really think about the cameras and all the millions of people watching you at home, but being interviewed, or doing live TV is entirely different. In the ring, you play to the crowd; it is their reaction you are trying to gauge, and of course, you want them to come back for more next time. That is why bouts were sometimes left open-ended, one or both fighters disqualified, for example. Everyone would want to come back to see the revenge match."

When the infrastructure of Joint Promotions first began to crumble in the early 1970s, Jarvis Astaire started buying up bits of it. He had started out by promoting boxing bouts during the Second World War before going into the management side of the game where he was involved with champions such as Billy Thompson, Terry Downes and Frank Bruno. He was also instrumental in bringing Muhammad Ali (or Cassius Clay as he was known then) to England in May 1966 to defend his title against Henry Cooper, and during the fight the American was knocked to the canvas for the very first time.

Jarvis had bought Dale and Martins as well as the British Wrestling Federation, but it didn't work out for him as he hoped it would. It was then that the wrestler Jackie Pallo started to plan a new group which included the Crabtree brothers and Jack Dale, but when Jack died, Joint hired Max, which left Jackie out in the cold and he wasn't best pleased.

Under Max's guidance Joint took on a brand-new look, and at this time, *World of Sport* was featuring quite a variety of wrestling talents. The biggest star of them all was about to arrive on the scene, and nobody could have believed it would be a blue-collared hero well past his prime who would revive the fortunes of the flailing business.

His amazingly colourful bouts of showmanship and glitter caught the imagination of children as well as the press. Despite the lack of real wrestling Big Daddy was drawing on the "showmanship" formulae which had first made wrestling popular, and such displays of power, coupled by the fact that he was being pushed by Max and the other bosses, put Shirley right up there on top of the pile after a time.

In 1974, the country was facing a fuel shortage, and when it all kicked off with the coal miners early in the year, and industrial action happened, they forced the government's hand. On New Year's Day a three-day working week was implemented, which of course affected live wrestling shows as well as recorded ones, and this went on until March. Although essential services such as hospitals and supermarkets were unaffected, the country fell into darkness for much of the time.

When the lights finally came back on normality was resumed, and 11 days later an oil embargo against the USA, Europe, and Japan ended, which made things all the sweeter, and had virtually no effect on Swedish pop group ABBA who won the Eurovision Song Contest with their hit 'Waterloo'. The changes that were occurring in the wrestling world were about to put a lot of people's noses out of joint, but not even Lord Lucan turning up and shouting "stop" could have stopped the pie-fuelled freight train about to plough straight through the middle of the business.

By July 1974, Shirley first started to appear as the heel Big Daddy Crabtree, or sometimes he would drop the surname, and the crowd took a while to get used to this new villain. Billed as a 25st blond giant he tagged with champion Bobby Ryan against Phil Pearson and Pork Chop Dean in Leicester that July, and they made mincemeat out of them. In October, he fought Tubby Hodgson in Wolverhampton but the transformation was not yet properly underway.

Within a couple of years, Shirley would turn from baddy to goody, winning over the crowd with his powerfully patriotic performances and he really pushed the gimmick and the publicity it created to the absolute limit. Having this ever-developing alter ego meant he was under increasing scrutiny from the public, and it took a bit of getting used to. At the beginning of the Daddy gimmick, he was still a stone or two short of what he weighed at his peak in popularity, and he was approaching his 45th birthday. Before the birth of Big Daddy in 1973, he had made just two appearances on the TV, and didn't appear at all the following year, so he was very much a wrestler making up the numbers at the time. His knockout by Kendo early in 1973 was followed by another defeat by Count Bartelli in July. Sometimes listed in TV magazines as Shirley Crabtree, and sometimes as Big Daddy, things were just about to change.

When Max got his feet under the table in 1974, he was slowly able to champion his brother's cause but Big Daddy did not appear on a televised bill until July 1975 as part of a tag team with Giant Haystacks. They were up against The Saints at Southport on 9 July and the show was broadcast ten days later. The week before this Shirley had recorded a fight under his own name, so it all came together quite quickly for him. An unsuspecting nation arrived at the beginning of a flabbergasting journey of extraordinary showmanship and glittery hype.

Out of all of this the superheavyweight division was born, and it went on for a generation before they'd had a gutful. With Max at the helm, and Brian as a "world-class" referee, when Shirley became the star they pretty much had the business sewn up. Wrestling being the cut-throat business that it was they knew they had to get in while the going was good. They did not know if things were sustainable, so they capitalised as much as possible, and nobody can deny them that. Business was business; there was no room for sentiment if the machine was to roll on, but there was a bit of room for a little more respect and understanding, and Max showed the least of this in his business affairs.

He wasn't the only one who could play the bad guy. If Shirley didn't like you he would let you know; he didn't suffer fools. There are those who say he would be as nice as pie to somebody one minute and start laying into them as soon as they left the room. A lot of what people said back then was bull, and sometimes separating the truth from the fiction is a task for a forensic detective.

There was only ever a central core of wrestlers in the organisation they could totally rely on, and Shirley knew who were the workers and grafters, and he knew the ones who liked to talk rubbish and he treated them accordingly. He wasn't one to say "look at me, I'm a star" but there were always going to be those who would try to knock his success, or twist the truth. Shirley wasn't constantly in the right, but he did try to keep a level head rather than thinking solely about the money.

Another story that suffered from an unfortunate case of Chinese whispers involves a wrestler called Hans Streiger, who many wrestlers were scared of. His real name was Clarke Mellor, and he was from Derbyshire rather than Germany. He was a real hardman, and the story goes that he turned up one night in the early 1980s, but he wasn't on the bill. All three of the Crabtree brothers were ringside and when Max refused to pay him for turning up, Streiger was reported to have hit both him and Brian, who was flying through the air at the time having jumped the ropes. All this was supposed to have happened while Shirley shied away, and such a distortion of the truth is very common in the retelling of wrestling tales and makes it extremely difficult to get to the truth at times.

Over the years, a layer of dislike for the Crabtrees has built up in many, and it has been allowed to fester, which is unfortunate but not totally unjustified. Cut from a live TV performance, the film of what really happened is now in a private collection, and the truth is that Shirley was in the ring with a wrestler called Scrubber Daly for a ladder match which was a match that used, unsurprisingly, a stepladder. There were other wrestlers stood around the apron so nobody could leave the ring, and just as the fight was about to begin, Shirley's eyes rose up as he saw Streiger walking towards him. He shouted at Streiger to get out as many of the wrestlers moved out of the way because they didn't want to get involved with whatever it was they were in the middle of.

Brian tried to grab Streiger around the waist as he advanced, but he shook him off and then head-butted another wrestler called Black Jack Mulligan. Shirley then lost it, grabbed Streiger by the scruff of the neck and frog-marched him out, much to the delight of the crowd who had no idea that what was going on was anything out of the ordinary.

New in 1975 was the Volkswagen Golf, the game show *Wheel of Fortune,* and Margaret Thatcher. The Iron Lady defeated Edward Heath to become the leader of the Conservative party in February, and she was rumoured to like a bit of wrestling, and in particular Big Daddy, or so she said when her office contacted him for a signed photo. From working-class roots the Daddy image was as identifiable to the man in the street as it is to a baron or prince, and you could relate to him like he was some kind of uncle as he had the same sort of homely warmth.

After the tag contest against The Saints, Shirley's next TV appearance was in Blackburn in September, and he was beaten once again by Kendo Nagasaki who was the bigger billed star at the time.

After finishing a show in Grimsby one night Shirley noticed an older woman hanging about after the show, and then she suddenly made a beeline for him. Her name was Nelly, and much to his disbelief she turned out to be his stepmother. She explained to him what had happened with his father since he had split from his mother, and where he had been all of these years. Shirley's mother never did marry again, and she spent the rest of her life surrounded by her sons, and was very proud of what they had achieved, but for Shirley senior things were different.

Nelly explained that the brothers had a half-brother called Jeremy, who was gradually accepted into the family after their parent's death. Nelly explained that their father was on his death bed, and that he wanted to see his boys before he died. This caused all sorts of mixed emotions and upheaval among the brothers who had been a long time without a father. Brian never knew him, he was one year old when he left, and he chose to keep it that way. Shirley and Max did go and see their old man, and this brought a bit of closure to the situation which must have been very awkward for them, but then life never did run exactly to plan.

One of Shirley's oddities was his passion for cold water, and was the reason why he could jump into the icy waters of Blackpool and save as many lives as he did. It wasn't all sunshine, leopard-skin trunks, and donkey rides on the beach though; every time he went into the sea, he risked his own life. He wasn't one to sit indoors watching *Coronation Street* or *Mr. & Mrs.* of a night either, he would often prefer a colder seat outside in the garden even in the coldest of weather under a freezing cold hosepipe. In the beginning, he started out with a child's paddling pool which he barely fitted in to, people would come knocking on the door for Jane and Paul, and postmen delivering packets exchanged pleasantries with him as he sat there in the cold water with a drink in his hand like he was in St Tropez during the ice age.

It would have been a rather bizarre sight to behold, especially when he became famous, and as his fame increased so did the size of his pools. In the end, nobody batted an eyelid. If you wanted to have a chat with him, he would probably be out in the front garden in the pool. Although he later had the money to build his own permanent fixture, he never did. There wasn't the room so over the years the paddling pools evolved until he acquired a rather nice one that was almost as good as a permanent one, barring a puncture of course.

Whatever was happening with his wrestling schedule he always had Sundays off in the winter, and he would often take a dip while people were de-icing their cars or gritting their paths, and there couldn't have been a great deal of crime going on in their street with Big Daddy doing neighbourhood watch. There were many opportunities to buy bigger and better properties on the outskirts of the village but that just wasn't him. Where they were the family were safe and that was his main worry. If any photos or interviews had to be done for the press or the TV, they were always done up at the farm.

The first televised wrestling of 1975 came from Bradford and saw heavyweight Bruno Elrington up against local boy Dennis Mitchell, who was disqualified. Also on the bill was Mick McManus who overcame York's Steve Best, and another local lad called Alan Dennison beat Robby Baron.

When Shirley teamed up with Haystacks in Southport in July 1975 against The Saints, it was the third time he had used the Big Daddy gimmick, and it was Haystacks's first TV appearance. The power and the size of these men blew everybody away so the running order of the night had to be carefully planned to give them the best exposure, and they were seen as a "monster heel tag team". They soon built a notorious reputation for crushing blue-eyes, and both men noticed that they were starting to get cheered after a while, and they knew they were on to something.

The idea also started to formulate that these two goliaths might do well going up against each other. Both were hot-headed and wanted their share of the limelight, but before the inevitable happened, they were involved in some great contests. They spent some of the summer fighting in singles matches too, and they were getting quite a following.

When Kendo lost his mask in a fight against Daddy the crowd were really cheering Shirley although Kendo won the fight. Gradually, he was becoming convinced that his new gimmick was strong enough to go it alone and that feuding with Haystacks would probably be better than teaming up with him so they gave it a go.

The first Daddy versus Haystacks fight happened in Digbeth at the end of July, and when Haystacks was disqualified the crowd went wild. The two men would continue teaming up for over 30 more matches, and this went on until the summer of 1977, which was when the blue touchpaper seemed to be lit for Big Daddy. The crowd wanted to see the big men battling it out against each other so that is exactly what they got.

Towards the end of June 1975, a state of emergency was declared in India by Prime Minister Indira Gandi, and all voting and civil liberties were suspended. Closer to home, in Keighley, Yorkshire, a woman called Ann Rogulskyj had a close escape with the Yorkshire Ripper Peter Sutcliffe, and was lucky to survive the maniac's wrath after he set upon her in a back alleyway with a hammer. After hitting her three times on the head he was about to stab her in the abdomen when he was disturbed and her life was spared. In a desperate 12-hour operation, she had to have splinters of bone removed from her brain and was administered the last rites but managed to pull through.

In August, he tried it once again in Halifax, the victim this time being a woman called Olive Smelt who survived because Sutcliffe was disturbed again. By the end of his killing spree, he had destroyed 13 people and was finally captured in 1981, and the paranoid schizophrenic was given 20 life sentences.

Although Brian's wrestling days were over, he did occasionally appear in tag matches and, after the Daddy v Haystacks fight, he teamed up with Shirley in Liverpool at the end of July. They were beaten by Kendo Nagasaki and George Gillette, and then the same happened again in mid-September.

A new wrestler called the Dynamite Kid was emerging in the north about this time, and he was seen as an exciting fresh prospect. His real name was Thomas Billington and, after starting out with Max he became part of the British Bulldogs tag team with the late Davey Boy Smith. They were successful in North America when the British scene died out. Known for their speed and acrobatics, they joined the WWF in 1984, and even had Ozzy Osbourne in their corner during WrestleMania 2. In the end, the two men fell out with each other, and their last contest was in 1990. Smith died of a heart attack in 2002 at the age of 39, and an autopsy revealed the abuse of anabolic steroids and human growth hormone caused his death. He was one of a growing number of wrestlers whose lives ended this way. The abuse of such substances was unheard of when Shirley was starting out but became widespread in the 1980s as American audiences expected to see ring supermen, and they had to have the perfect body.

> *"Despite our business being superseded by what is going on in America, I have to say I do like what they do, and if it is on the TV I will sit down and watch it. It is terrible what happened to Davey Boy, and I know a lot of other wrestlers went that way. There were no steroids in our day, we were natural bodybuilders and we put on size by training hard and eating properly. In the late 1960s and early 1970s you first started to see these monster-men appearing, and although people like Arnold Schwarzenegger and Sergio Olivia displayed amazing physiques, it was quite obvious to me that what they were doing wasn't natural. And besides, what good would have steroids been to Big Daddy? In our day, wrestlers were hard men who took a lot of punishment and injury meant a snapped finger or a broken nose, not a pulled muscle or a broken nail. I suppose ultimately the spectacle of wrestling was always going to be Americanised; it had to get bigger and better if it was going to keep the paying public interested. All things must pass and be forgotten, and we will too one day."*

Christmas 1975 was a busy time for Shirley whose schedule went crazy. He appeared as Daddy more than 60 times as the year came to an end but his metamorphosis was not yet complete. He climbed into his spandex chrysalis night after night and threw himself about the ring like a man half of his age and size. By the autumn of 1976, he would be transformed, and he would emerge into the bright lights stretching his wings. Gone were the dowdy dressing gowns and terrible leotards; replaced by a glittery cape, and then a top hat and a union flag jacket. He visited every town and city of significance in the country as he established himself.

That summer in 1975 was extremely hectic. At one point he appeared in Liverpool, Rhyl, Cleethorpes and Arbroath in four days, and drove home every night. He also enjoyed appearing in Blackpool once again, and there were colourful bouts against characters such as Mad Axeman, Big Bruno, and Chief War Eagle.

At the end of November, Shirley beat Mike Marino at the Royal Albert Hall in a bloody battle which left his opponent covered in claret, just like Henry Cooper on that famous night at Highbury against Muhammad Ali. Marino wasn't the biggest fan of Shirley and at the time he was acting as a matchmaker for Dale and Martins and he made sure Shirley was relegated to the second division in terms of the opponents he faced. This went on until Shirley's fame forced a rethink. Before all of this Marino won the rematch in early 1979, and for good measure he also defeated Mick McManus on the same night.

Chapter Eleven

We Could Be Heroes

IT IS as easy to see why the crowd took to the Big Daddy/
Giant Haystacks tag team, as it is to see them laughing at
people dressed in pantomime frocks, and you could argue that
the audiences for both types of show were very much identical –
or at least of the same mind. There were probably more blood-
thirsty pensioners and older kids clutching Marvel comics at the
wrestling, starry-eyed and looking up at the pages as they came to
life. Superheroes in the flesh so to speak.

The gimmicks and special moves made it all the more real, and
Daddy could have pulled off a credible *The Thing,* and Kendo in
full headgear could have passed for *Iron Man.* They were all there
for the spectacle; even if the performances were sometimes rather
comical and could have been out of an old slapstick film. Like
Laurel and Hardy pushing a piano up a hill, or dancing around
with their arses on fire. A mix of laughter and anger occurred
naturally in the crowd, and often in quick succession.

In all seriousness, the two big men also showed great power,
and they were value for money at the time. In those early tag
matches it seems like Shirley was the more mobile of the two,
or perhaps Haystacks was the bigger star at that point which
meant Shirley had to work harder. He certainly took a lot of the
falls, and he knew how to work the crowd too. Haystacks would
stand there glaring at them, like he hated the world, and that

they could all go and die, which wasn't anything like his real-life persona.

The two men were a product of their time, and that is not to say they wouldn't make it nowadays on the modern circuit in America, but their personas and gimmicks would be nothing different to what has gone before. Martin had a brief venture into American wrestling as Loch Ness before being diagnosed with cancer, but in today's oversaturated world there is every type of character, from superheroes to bad guys, in many different colours and creeds.

As John Lennon once said, "there's nothing you can do that can't be done", but you can of course be the first to do it, or make it popular once again for another generation. It is difficult to pinpoint the appeal of the two super-heavyweights but they both looked the part, and they caught the imagination of course.

The hilarity of Shirley's home-made costumes is something worth revisiting, and the truth is he still didn't have two ha'pennies to rub together. The stories about Eunice cutting up the cushions on the sofa, or pulling down the curtains to accessorise what Shirley was wearing, are dead right. Dressed in that kind of clobber he would run at his opponent. There would be a swagger in his movement, just before he knocked the guy to the ground with his gut, before sticking in the boot, which delighted the crowd who really started to take to him.

All of this was only surpassed by the way the two men warmed up which was like a disturbance along the San Andreas Fault. A long time before the All Blacks' Haka war dance became known in Great Britain, or the pop group Los Del Rio released their seminal hit 'The Macarena', the super-heavyweights had the moves. It was like watching two dodgem cars meeting head-on time and again. They would strut around the ring in the kind of boots you could have slipped the back legs of a sheep into if you loosened the laces, and that would be that.

Forces of nature captured beneath the cameras for the viewer at home to enjoy. There would be Shirley shouting his mouth off, pointing, and waving his arms about like he was conducting an orchestra of schizophrenics, really working up the crowd. Then it would happen; they would grab hold of each other by the wrists and bump stomachs together repeatedly, and many an opponent got in the way during a match. Like insects crushed in a Venus flytrap they would usually end up on the floor gasping for breath, hoping the stars they were seeing would soon fade.

The outcome of the fights may have been fixed, but this didn't mean a double belly-butt wasn't going to hurt. Having your head slammed into the corner-post could be enlightening, a "moment of clarity" when many wrestlers wondered why they had chosen to do what they were doing for a living. There were those who had boxed and stepped down, and others who hadn't made it as a pro boxer, but once upon a time fighters chose to wrestle legitimately, maybe picking the grapple game over boxing. By the time Max's reign at Joint Promotions had begun this level footing was long gone; the emphasis had shifted from genuine strongmen and fighters to that of showmen who were more used to entertaining, but there were still some very strong men entering the wrestling ring. People like Les Kellett who revelled in the hardman image, and he frightened the bejesus out of many a man.

In their early bouts Shirley and Martin were regularly booed but all of this changed as they became more established, although still their moves looked vicious and villainous. During those tag contests old ladies in tortoise-shell glasses regularly got up from their seats clutching handbags and knitting sticks. They knew how to give a bit of needle as many a wrestler will confirm. They were often seen giving the bad guy "what for" as they were swept away by the occasion and the spectacle of a live show. Sometimes they needed to be led back to their seats, and the half-knitted bobble hat they had thrown to the ground in disgust.

It wasn't just the kids and the Sex Pistols who were on the point of rioting; anarchy in the UK included the pensioners, and the blue rinse wasn't a million miles away from a green mohican. Armed with a walking stick, or a Zimmer frame with wing mirrors, they proved they could be right out there on the front line like the kids scrapping on Brighton beach, or at Mississippi University when there was something worth fighting for.

> *"People wonder what it feels like to be the bad guy in the ring. This may surprise you; it feels beautiful. The way my mind was as a young man, I used to take great pleasure in being hated. I had a wonderful sense of superiority and reckoned I could take on anyone. If the whole audience had come at me, I believed I could have handled it – and sometimes they almost did. As I left the ring, they would burn me with cigarettes, kick me, hit me with handbags and umbrellas, and I didn't give a damn. I just felt elated. I saw myself as a kind of Titan, a Hercules alone against the world."*

As The Guardsman, or The Giant Guardsman, Shirley appeared on some big bills, just as he did when he was fighting under his own name. Wrestling independently, he had become used to being top of the bill but many of the posters from when he rejoined Joint show that he was usually second or third down the list. By 1974, his Busby-wearing days were over as the idea of joining up with Haystacks first came about. By July 1975, Shirley fought several times as Big Daddy Crabtree, and as Big Daddy.

The first tag match with Haystacks was on 9 July and it was filmed for TV. They fought against the St Clair brothers, Roy and Tony, in Southport, and they were disqualified. It is strange to see Shirley's early performances as "Bad Daddy" when we look at him later on. In terms of quality and work-rate these were Daddy's golden days; his diet consisted of body bulk mixed with egg and double cream. He would also put glucose powder in Lucozade and when he laid the table there would be every vitamin tablet you could think of. This made sure that the extra weight was there, but it seems bizarre to think of a sportsman doing such a thing as part of a training regime.

Apart from the scoffing, he still trained every day with weights and a 14st life-sized Olympic dummy. If he hadn't have done that there would have been no way he could have done what he did being the size that he was, and as he got older it was perhaps his mental toughness which stopped him from listening to what his body was trying to tell him.

Bob Sweeney did the right thing all of those years ago when he quit, and while he didn't become famous like Shirley, he certainly made his name and money and he lived much longer than the man he used to look up to. When it all started to kick off for Shirley as Big Daddy he wasn't far off his 50th birthday, which is a time most men start to think about slowing down a bit. The biggest problem was that there was no way out of the manic 24/7 lifestyle, there was no way he could have walked away from it, and if he had have done the empire would have crumbled earlier. You cannot help wondering whether he paid a high price for his fame by burning his life force more quickly than he should have done.

The transformation into a blue-eyed crowd favourite was pretty much complete by Christmas 1976, but nobody could have predicted he would get as famous as he did, and it all went stratospheric very quickly indeed. With Haystacks as his tag team partner, they had some fantastic contests against Kendo and Rex Strong, and Tibor Szakacs and Steve Veidor in April 1976. That match ended with Daddy being pushed through the ropes where he was caught by Haystacks outside the ring, and the crowd were going absolutely crazy.

There were some good moments, but in the end their partnership became a little too much, and Shirley was starting to grow tired of being spat at. It was decided that having them fight each other was a far more measured contest, but they steam-rolled through tag teams quite merrily for a good while yet, even though they didn't always win. Their technique was all about using their size; a classic move would see one of them chop their opponent to the ground before they stomped on them.

Throughout 1976 and 1977 the cheering crowds really started to register, and although both characters were popular not even Max could have predicted just how big his older brother would become. What he did know is that splitting them up meant he now had two similar super-heavyweight shows, which would of course give him the chance to double the takings.

As 1977 wore on they started to face each other in the ring more and more as the feuding began. Shirley teamed up with wrestlers such as Kung-Fu, Johnny Saint, and Bobby Ryan, while it appears as if Haystacks tagged with whoever was down that week, and he was usually on the receiving end of another defeat or disqualification. Thus, the balance of power changed; as Shirley became more influential, his tag partners had to be hand-picked, if not then Daddy's matches looked bad.

With men so large there were always going to be limitations on what they could do physically so the balance in such a tag match had to be right. It was only later when Shirley became less mobile that the balance was lost, but usually the necessary excitement was created, and people left at the end of the night happy customers.

In the end it did all become stale, and Shirley's limited repertoire meant he could no longer get away with things, but during the years leading up to the peak of his fame his fights were arguably the best he was involved in as Daddy. If he teamed up with a younger, more agile fighter such as Tony St Clair for example, St Clair would add the necessary skill and style to the performance before Shirley finished it off with his power.

And that was the deal really, other wrestlers put in the acrobatics which made the performances look good, but of course, it was Big Daddy the crowd had come to see. His entrance and ringside shenanigans were half of the fun and if you came to see one of his performances you had to view it as showmanship. If you were looking for technical ability, you would be sadly disappointed. The fact is people came away from one of Big Daddy's wrestling bouts feeling pleased.

Each week Max and the minds around him were thinking up more and more elaborate tricks and gimmicks to keep things fresh for the punters; they wanted them to come back next time they were in town. There were ladder matches and arm-wrestling contests, and it was all designed to give the crowd a bit of variety.

In the end, it was decided that a feud between Daddy and Haystacks would be for the best, and by doing this Martin's fame was heightened almost to the level Shirley achieved. Their relationship may have become strained at times, but both men had a mutual respect and understanding for one another. After all, without the other man, they would not have become the cult figures they are today. There are no other bouts from that era of British wrestling that live as long in the memory as those between Big Daddy and Giant Haystacks.

It was when All-Star Promotions became part of the *World of Sport* family in 1976 that the Daddy figure was introduced to a national audience, and he was pushed to the top of the card as a "mega face". In the end, wherever you saw a wrestling poster or magazine article, there was Big Daddy. Such was his fame, he outshone other ring stars that complied with the stereotypical image of a muscleman superhero as portrayed by Sylvester Stallone in the *Rocky* movies, or Schwarzenegger in *Conan the Barbarian*.

It was Shirley's hulking frame that people wanted to see and there was a certain level of Santa Claus joviality that he had to maintain especially in front of kids. They had to feel that at any given moment he may do something fantastic. He had an appeal like the grandfather from the Werther's Original adverts, and of course had the knees to match, which was a million miles away from the superhero image.

Daddy was a man of action who battled Johnny Cougar in comic book land, and he was always ready to give the Bosch a jolly good thrashing. At his peak the adulation became a little overwhelming; letters and postcards (which had steadily started to come in throughout 1975 and 1976) soon started to arrive by the sackful, and it was Brian who said having Shirley as a brother at that time was like being related to Santa.

There was always a cheer and a smile for the crowd though. He would emerge from the dressing rooms cloaked in the Union flag and the image was an instant hit. When the Falklands War was on, he even donned a helmet in recognition of the British troops. He was just the right size to fit into the psyche of the nation, and he was soon as accepted as *Coronation Street*, Larry Grayson, Lassie, and Queen.

By November 1978, the more conservative costumes of the early Daddy period had bitten the dust, and he has was wearing a glittery cape and top hat as his costumes became ever more professional-looking as a local dressmaker took over from Eunice. Daddy was being booked against all the top heels, and he soon began to make his ring entrance to The Seekers' hit 'We Shall Not Be Moved' as air horns sounded and Union flags were waved. Despite the tacky feeling of a dilapidated seaside resort, the atmosphere at the venues was electric, and as Daddy, Shirley was an imposing figure who people would want to come back and see time and again.

With Max at the helm the Crabtrees became a formidable force in Britain and Europe, although Shirley would now concentrate his performances exclusively on Britain. At the time there were all sorts of different championship belts floating around and the committee who awarded the most prestigious of these were unwilling to give any to Daddy because of his limited repertoire.

In response to this Joint created their own belt for him, and it was all part of the show. Not only was Shirley now recognised in the street as Big Daddy, he became the mythical champion of all mankind, and you can almost hear Max saying to him as he hands him the belt: "'Ere you are kid, you're the fucking mythical champion of all mankind, put down that Eccles cake and get out there and give 'em a show."

All manner of big lads were trying to get in on the action in the super-heavyweight division, but none of them got anywhere near the following of Daddy and Haystacks. Gone were the technical days, and a thing of the past were the downright nasty days where people wanted to hurt and maim. These shows were now stage shows and performers had to be ever more colourful and inventive if they wanted to share a bit of the limelight.

There were gimmicks such as Catweazle, and Peter "Tally Ho" Cane with his bugle and riding hat. There was also Gargantua, Kid Chocolate, Wild Angus, and of course Skull Murphy. Each tapped into some kind of stereotypical image and captured the mood of the public. And if Shirley had been able to make the cross-over into TV presentation when the chance arose, maybe those last few painful years of Big Daddy as a wrestler could have been avoided, and his life may have even been prolonged. He certainly went on wrestling for way too long, and would ignore warnings about his health. Max was forced to remortgage the farm later as his empire dissolved, but it was loyalty to his brother that kept Shirley performing, and he knew that without him, the crowds would not come.

Max would never let anybody top his brother in the ring when he became famous, but if he had let it happen it would have certainly made things a little more realistic. And if Shirley had quit when TV wrestling finished in 1988, it would have certainly been kinder, and he could have still been involved on the apron as a manager like Gorgeous George. Daddy would have been there to sort out any trouble, and could have acted as a mentor to a British wrestler designed for an American audience.

Leaving England to compete in America was never really an option for Shirley, especially when he got towards the end of his career; he just wanted to enjoy the simple things in life. Max was convinced he could get things restarted in Britain when the TV did finally go, and nobody was even thinking about America. He may well have tried to push Shirley in that direction if he had been younger and in better health, but in the end it wasn't to be.

Big Daddy's dominance in Britain made other top wrestlers look at places with a large wrestling followings such as America,

Canada, Japan, and Mexico. In reviving the business and putting Daddy at the top of the pile the Crabtrees enjoyed a prolonged spell in control. The problem was, and especially with some of Daddy's later and less credible performances, British wrestling became a laughing stock. It was quickly consigned to history, put in the same vault as *Carry On* films, Alf Garnett, and thermionic valves as people tried to act all sophisticated with their Tupperware, trim-phones, and digital watches.

Wrestling was a product of an era of simple pleasures, and when its true nature was spelled out to an ever-awakening general public it all but died out. Max's regime did not plan for the future which was rather short-sighted for a man of such ability. All the money went straight to the promoters, very little went to the wrestlers, and nothing was invested in the future. As a consequence, when the curtain did finally fall on Shirley's career the British scene also became obsolete. With no real power the professional organisations that survived concentrated on the holiday camp circuit which was their biggest source of revenue.

When Johnny Kincaid started teaming up with Dave Butcher Bond in 1978, the two black fighters formed an explosive partnership. Their matches were aggressive and the fighters themselves were not liked, and this being the 1970s there was a lot of racial abuse too. Some nights it felt like the bad old days, the crowd was so riled up it seemed like they were going to riot such was the atmosphere. In the end, Joint had to split them up, which was a shame because their fights were exciting and acrobatic.

In March, Kung-Fu defeated and de-masked Kendo at the Royal Albert Hall and this performance, at such a prestigious venue, had a different look to the shows that had gone before. As Daddy, Shirley had first appeared at the venue in November 1975. Despite beating Mike Marino, his initial performances there were regarded as pretty poor, so something had to be done to beef things up.

A rematch with Kendo Nagasaki was arranged at the venue in November 1976 and it was decided that the bout would be a little different to the other ten they had fought against each other in the last five or six weeks. While they didn't want the fight to appear as if it was descending into chaos, they were going to push things to the limits. They knew the pensioners and kids were going to go absolutely berserk but there really wasn't much of a chance of them starting a riot.

> *"We met again at the Royal Albert Hall towards the end of the year, and the action was equally explosive and both of us were disqualified after the bout spilled out of the ring and at the feet of the people in the front row of seats. In the exchanges, I had that mask off again and the promoters decided that the only solution was a lumberjack return match with other wrestlers policing the ropes to make sure we stayed inside the ring. This took place in January 1977 and was even more violent than before, and from the first bell rules counted for nothing. Either of us could have been disqualified but much to my disappointment, it was I who was sent out, leaving Nagasaki a highly unpopular winner. At that point Haystacks, who was then my tag partner, joined in the melee in the ring."*

Although Shirley had played some villainous characters his ring personality was essentially neutral and that started to change as Daddy got cheered. When tagging with Haystacks they were usually fighting against the good guys; and it took until the middle of 1977 for Daddy to become the blue-eyed good guy everybody remembers. With his stomach hanging out and his hands waving high he would enter the packed auditorium shouting "hallo" as the music kicked in. It was then that it felt like a comic book hero had been lifted straight out of the pages of *Tiger* and set down in semi-darkness in red, white, or blue.

With the immortal words "Sock it to em" emblazoned across the arse of his leotard he carried children to the ring, or pushed wheelchairs, and there is a story that he once left a disabled kid ringside without any sign of the carers and it was all caught on camera. The intention to do good was there, but he wasn't perfect. In becoming the kids' hero he cemented himself a place in many people's hearts, and if we ignore the cynics we can remember that Shirley did a lot for kids' charities and organisations in the little bit of spare time that he did have for himself. Any time he didn't spend wrestling he was at home with the family, and he didn't like to be disturbed.

In these paranoiac times of falsehood and spin-doctoring, it is easy to see every act he did as something that was purely for the cameras. The truth is Shirley was famous enough, and he was earning decent money. Unbelievably, Dale and Martins' wage lists from 1987/88 show that Max was only paying him £50 a night, or £60 for a TV event, although Shirley would sign between 200 and 500 autographs a night at a quid apiece. He also sold other merchandise, and made a decent nightly wage and it is surprising that he did not get a cut of the gate money.

His mentality was not just about money, although he really should have commanded a greater basic wage considering the amount of tickets he sold by just being on the bill. There was also a little girl called Kerry Froggart, who was very ill when Shirley went to visit her, and she wasn't the only one. He helped to raise a lot of money for organisations such as Children in Need, and people who accuse him of it all being a front come up short when you realise how much of his valuable time he gave up for free.

As we know Shirley did not live an exuberant life filled with fast cars and champagne so it wasn't all done for the money and fame. He really did enjoy being Big Daddy, although some days he got pissed off, and you might have been unlucky enough to kop an unfortunate one if you happened to be in the ring with him at that time. He must have felt like the Pied Piper without a flute, and there were days when he felt like turning around and sticking his two fingers up at it all. He certainly filled the screen in a different way to other kids' favourites of the day such as Tom Baker as

Doctor Who, footballer Kevin Keegan, and *Blue Peter* presenter Lesley Judd.

It was in 1977 that Daddy's unbeaten run in the ring started, and of course it went on until the end of his career. Before that, defeat was not uncommon, like when he teamed up with his brother Brian in July 1976, and they were defeated by Kendo and George. In July 1977, before his undefeated run began, Shirley was given the chance of having a crack at Joint's version of the British title, but he lost to Tony St Clair in one of his last defeats. There were also a couple of defeats against Haystacks in singles matches, and this all leading up to March 1977, when the two big men teamed up for the last time and faced Kendo and Rex Strong. It was then that Haystacks turned against Daddy much to the crowd's dismay, and he hit him over the head with a chair which of course started their feud.

Chapter Twelve

Monte Carlo Or Bust

BECAUSE OF his hectic lifestyle, Shirley pretty much lived for the summer holidays, and as the money got better so did the destinations. A wet weekend in Blackpool or Bognor was no longer the highlight of the year. Camping on the Dales in a gale he could be stuck where the sun didn't shine, which could have been anywhere local. Seafront strolls were now achievable in an hour or two, all he had to do was put his foot down and the burnt-orange Mark II Granada with its 2.8-lire engine would leap into life like a DeLorean.

They would enjoy many days away from Halifax, and once he had the car he decided the time was right for a European tour of their own. Those summers of the late 1970s and early 1980s were a million miles away from the powdered egg days of the Second World War.

For the first time in his life he had the money to do whatever he wanted, and this was a happy time for the family who got very exuberant indeed. They visited places like Nice, Lourdes, Biarritz, Venice, and later they went on the *QE2* to New York. Before the trip to Monte Carlo, Shirley was so excited he made a special trip to Leeds for a new tracksuit and a couple of pairs of pants and to him, this was like a visit to Harrods. Fortunately, he did not suffer from the delusion that slip-on shoes worked with a tracksuit like so many men of his age and generation. Instead, he wore size 13

Adidas trainers which were just about big enough for a small tribe of pygmies to use as canoes.

This was about as sophisticated and fashionable as it got for Shirley, and they left behind the cool, dull British summers with the soft tones of Boney M's 'Daddy Cool' blaring away on the eight-track. Later he got a tape deck but there was a real sense of excitement in the air as they anticipated that feeling of first seeing the sea on the horizon as they headed for the ferry and the continent beyond. Once, in Monte Carlo, the kids were having a go at windsurfing but Jane got the hump when she kept falling off, and she ended up having a row with her dad as kids do. It wasn't so much an argument; she was just pissed off with her own ability, so she stormed off and dived into the sea to cool off, while her ex-lifeguard father kept an eye on her as she swam out.

From the shore, she could hear him shouting to her as she swam further out than she normally would have done, but she was a good swimmer and didn't feel like she was in any danger. When he called to her again she shouted back "I'm not talking to you" but by now Shirley was getting into the water and heading towards her like a powerboat. As she swam out of the harbour she had failed to see the shoal of jellyfish she was heading right into, but Shirley got to her just in time as people watched the drama unfold from the shore. When he got out of the water Jane was safely in his arms, but he was covered in stings, and he had lacerations across his legs and his back, which must have been really painful.

Apparently, people had been told to watch out for jellyfish but the family never received the news, and when he climbed out a medical table had already been set up, and he headed straight for it, more concerned about Jane than himself. As he sat there and waited, he noticed a man stood over him blocking out the sun and he looked very familiar.

"This fella was offering me his hand when he said 'Big Daddy, Shirley Crabtree, I presume', and as I took it all in, suddenly I realised who he was. I

replied 'Billy Graham, I presume' and we laughed, and I exchanged pleasantries with the world famous American evangelist who was also a spiritual advisor to Presidents Eisenhower and Nixon. Billy had also preached with Martin Luther King when they were trying to get equal rights, and he said he had actually put up the bail money to get him out of jail. You can imagine Eunice's face when I introduced her to Billy, even though we never went to church, we were believers; my mother had been quite religious in her own way, and she would sometimes go. I suppose she was praying for a miracle… It didn't help that Eunice was sunbathing topless when she met Billy Graham in Monte Carlo. Her face went as red as a tomato when she saw the preacher and her hands couldn't move quick enough to put on her bikini top, but Billy raised his own hands in a biblical sort of fashion and told her not to worry. By now, I was trying hard not to laugh, and then Billy said something about being born in the nude, and going out the same way, and I think she just wanted the earth to open up and swallow her whole right then and there."

While they were in Monte Carlo in 1984, Shirley was given the chance to purchase an apartment for around £8,000, and it was situated right next door to Orson Welles's pad. Although he did not take up the offer, he often looked back and wondered what it would have been worth years later. You can almost imagine Orson sat there on the balcony in his slippers and silk dressing gown, slowly turning the page of his newspaper as he stirred his tea. At that moment in time, his eyes drift upwards over the newspaper and straight at Eunice Crabtree's tits. With her curlers in her hair and smoking a fag, the director of *Citizen Kane* and *The Magnificent Ambersons* would not have known where to look as she applied her suntan lotion. Not wanting to offend, he would have probably averted his gaze, allowing his eyes to settle instead on the bronzed stomach of the man sat beside her sipping fresh orange juice and smiling back at him.

None of this ever happened of course. It would not have been pleasant for Orson, and besides, Shirley wouldn't have fitted in among a load of posh film actors and directors all poncing around like they were something special. Apart from meeting Billy Graham, the most elaborate he got when he was abroad was when they went to the Cannes Film Festival and they bumped into Demis Roussos just as they were heading back to the hotel after a long hot day in the sun. They were all absolutely knackered, and just wanted to rest and freshen up. Suddenly, the press were shouting "Big Daddy" as they paired him up with Demis like little and large and started snapping a load of pictures.

With time, Shirley learned how to deal with the media, but there were no airs and graces on display, he saved that for the Queen. Give him pie, chips, and a saveloy wrapped in newspaper and that was him. Then, perhaps a walk along Blackpool seafront in between the showers and he would be as happy as a pig in shit. While Orson and his mates probably got chauffeured around Monte Carlo in limousines and Rolls Royces, there in the car park was Shirley's Granada, and he wouldn't have swapped it for the world. The registration plate read A800 NEW and the front always pointed upwards because he carried his weights and dumbbells around with him in the boot wherever he went.

That particular holiday almost ended in disaster when Eunice got the dates wrong. After leaving Dover they went to the south of France, before moving on to Switzerland, Venice, and Vienna where they arrived a day early. It was one of those rare occasions when Shirley lost his cool at Eunice's mistake, and he went bananas because they had paid for another night in their previous hotel. The whole family was trying not to laugh as he drove along the motorway, but he was absolutely fuming. Suddenly, he turned to Eunice and asked her for one of her cigarettes, and when he lit it and spluttered like a school kid puffing away at his first smoke, they could contain themselves no longer.

Shirley had never smoked before, and he looked absolutely ridiculous, almost as bad as when he tried a drop of beer. He had drunk probably half a can of Heineken before getting in the bath that day and he was absolutely smashed. When Jane's friends came around he was laying up there splashing around in the water like a wounded walrus and singing at the top of his voice, which was very embarrassing.

When they turned up at the hotel reception in Vienna a day early they were not able to change the booking. Shirley had all of his weights and dumbbells with him in a scene somewhat reminiscent of a *Carry On* film. With half a gymnasium at his feet, he was glaring at the porters as if to say "pick the frigging stuff up" but of course, they were not going to play. He ended up picking it all up himself and storming out of the hotel lobby shouting: "Eunice, I'm never coming on holiday with you again!"

> *"A holiday for me is a time of relaxation, and we used to enjoy them very much. We usually went as a family but now and again, it would just be me and Eunice, especially when Jane was older. The trip to New York on the QE2 was one of the best things we did together, but I did like to go away and take Jane. They used to take the mickey because I still trained on holiday, and I usually took my weights, but it was still relaxing for me. I'd do a bit of training and then have a swim in the sea before laying in the sun to read a book – you have to understand that it was getting away from the grind of the wrestling world that I was after, and we had some great times."*

Imagine if you will all 24st of Shirley jogging along Boulevard Louis II in Monte Carlo kitted out like he had just robbed Fred Perry's tennis shop. It wasn't the sweat pants and shirt, or even the hiking boots which made him look ridiculous and led the gendarmes to think he may have been some kind of a threat to national security. It was the balaclava that nearly got him arrested as he tried to convince them in pidgin English that he was not a terrorist.

He was shouting: "Na mate; I'm training; I'm trying to get a sweat on; I'm not up to nowt." In the end, the policeman threw his arms in the air and made some kind of statement about Englishmen being crazy. Shirley finally got his chance to show the family *The Sound of Music* country when they broke down near the lake at Heidelberg in Germany, which was used in the film. He put the time they were there to good use by going for a swim and enjoyed the occasion and the vastness of it all, while the rest of the family huddled together and waited for the recovery truck to arrive. And of course, there was a reconstruction of that famous scene with Julie Andrews where she pelts it down the hill singing 'The Hills Are Alive'. This time it was done by a rather rotund Yorkshireman in a bright red Adidas tracksuit, and the only saving grace was the fact that there was a Ford garage at the bottom of the hill.

Although intrusion was very rare there were a number of occasions when the press came calling. Many of the tabloids depend on scandal to sell newspapers, and as we have seen so many times, they don't always print the truth. The recent phone-tapping scandal in Britain has seen a lot of heads roll, as well as the demise of the *News of the World*. Reporter George Dearsley was freelancing for the *Sunday People* when he was sent to investigate a story about Eunice being a lesbian. In Millbank, she had a couple of strange friends, not eccentric like Brian's wife Sue's friends who were artist types; strange because they were a lesbian couple living together which, by today's standards, is nothing unusual at all. Back in the 1970s such a relationship still raised a few eyebrows and when the word got about that Eunice visited them you can imagine that tongues did wag.

There was never any evidence of there being anything more than a friendship, and one thing that is certain is that Eunice and

Shirley were very much in love despite everything that went on. When the reporters came up to the cottage to ask Shirley if his wife was sleeping with other women they were confronted by a very angry man indeed. How dare they come to his house and ask such questions, and he chased them off his property with his dogs.

This was not the last physical encounter he would have with the press at his front door, and this was unfortunately the price he had to pay for his fame. He had to put in long hours and lots of miles to get to where he was so his time off was crucial. You can imagine how it felt when that was intruded upon, and for no good reason. His and his family's private lives were nobody else's concern; all Shirley wanted was a bit of peace and quiet. Was that too much to ask for?

When she was sober Eunice was the nicest woman you could meet although she would rather try to buy somebody's affection, rather than earn it. One thing that was remarkable was the fact that however smashed she was, Shirley's supper would always be sat there in the oven waiting, although it was usually burned or stuck to the plate.

It is never a pleasant sight seeing a drunken woman staggering about, and watching Eunice in her silver fox fur coat was pretty sad. She had a nasty habit of flashing around wads of notes which she would carry about in a money bag. On a few occasions, she was even robbed, and one time she woke up on the floor in the street, she was a complete nightmare. She was robbed, and she didn't even know until the next day when all her money and jewellery were gone. The sad thing is Shirley was totally oblivious to it all. She would hide bottles of drink all around the house and when Shirley found one, he would not be happy. It was not an ideal way to live, but it was a way to live, and when the times were good, they were very pleasurable indeed.

With Shirley on the road so much it was boredom which led to the drinking, and a lot of things happened between the wives when the men were away on the road. That is not to say there was a repeat of what went on with Shirley's ex-wife Sally and Beryl when they ran away to Paris, and whatever did happen between the individual couples was their own private business and was kept strictly to themselves. If Shirley and Eunice were arguing, or there was a row up at the farm with Max and Beryl, the others would not interfere. Beryl was the life and soul of the party; she could drink anybody under the table and still not look like she was pissed.

After a session at Eunice's cottage she could run a car full of kids back up the hill to the farm without crashing into a ditch. A lot of the time the women were sat around at home waiting, especially if the men were down south and would be gone for a while. Beryl started to come over to the cottage of an evening with a load of drink and to be honest Eunice had never really drunk before. Of course, she had been around clubs, pubs, and booze in her professional career, but she wasn't one to get drunk with Shirley being a tee-totaller. The problem was that she could not handle her drink and shouldn't have been allowed to drink at all. She became completely psychotic when she was inebriated, and some of the things she would go on to do were like events out of a soap opera. She threatened people, and had thrown a whole night's taking out of the car window and on to the motorway one time. She even shot Shirley in the head with a BB gun.

Jane remembers coming home one night to see her dad sat up at the table eating his tea. The pellet from the gun had grazed his head rather than embedding itself into one of the fleshy parts like his eye; all was then quiet because Eunice had gone somewhere. Shirley had blood streaming down his face, and after Jane had helped clean up the wound, they started to wonder exactly where she had got to. As time passed she still hadn't returned so they went out and searched all the usual haunts without any success. Returning home they suddenly thought about Shirley's gym next door to the house. Entering the dark space, they found Eunice curled up in a big cardboard box asleep, and they could not help laughing as she protested and told them all to go away. In the end Shirley simply put her over his shoulder and carried her to bed.

There are usually emotional barriers which keep a person's behaviour in check, a set of "norms", but when Eunice was pissed on sherry those barriers could be quickly destroyed. There was nothing she would not do or say, and she tried to play everybody off against each other so there was never really the peace and quiet harmony Shirley craved.

The love he received was a very tough love indeed, and one day Jane turned around to him during the lull in the middle of one of their crazy arguments, and she asked him why he did not go out and get himself another bird. Giving her one of his big smiles he told her that he had another two, and then he pointed at the canaries in their cage. That was the way it was, he loved Eunice despite all the pain she went on to cause right up to the very last weeks of his life. His mother had been a tough old bird, who would keep her sons in check with a yard broom if she needed to, and I suppose Eunice's crazy behaviour was just accepted by him too; it was as if Shirley needed a dominant female character in his life.

The women would have a jolly old time with Beryl on the pale ale, and Eunice on the QC sherry. Jane looked upon Max's son Scott as a brother and when the women ran out of drink, they would send them over to the Anchor pub for more supplies, which they didn't mind doing because the money they made on the empties usually paid for a bag of crisps and a bottle of Coke.

The sad fact of the matter was that the two women used to get so drunk that they were incapable of looking after the kids who were allowed to run wild while the older ones minded the babies. The worst stories were ones about Eunice having other men in, but it is true to say the kids never saw anything like that. Eunice was, to say the least, a little eccentric, and if you stuck a few drinks inside of her, she could go off like a rocket even at Shirley, who absolutely hated it when she was pissed.

All of their arguments happened when she was in drink, and she would turn around and spit at them: "I'll buy and sell every fucking one of ya!" You can imagine how it sometimes turned nasty. The truth is Shirley had a short fuse and there are stories which talk about him getting physical with Eunice, but his nature was not one of a woman-beater. In fact, he was the exact opposite and there is a distinctive difference between manhandling an intoxicated woman and beating her, and if Shirley had done this to Eunice she would have ended up in a far worse state. It was her who would fly at him in a drunken rage when all he wanted was a bit of peace on his one day off.

It is sad to think that a lot of the time, there would be real dread inside of him at the prospect of returning home. The only saving grace when Eunice was like this was Jane, and later when she got married Shirley would spend a lot of time at her house rather than face the wrath of the missus. The kids were always told to be mindful of their dad's image, but his wife was staggering around the village in a drunken rage a good deal of the time.

Although she liked a session, Eunice wasn't an alcoholic; she was more of a binge drinker. She wasn't one of those who needed to drink as soon as she woke up, it was more to put some excitement and add a bit of colour to the rather humdrum existence of village life. The problem was that she didn't know when to stop, and one of the worst things she did was in the early 1990s when she sent a deepest sympathies card to her son Paul's wedding. She paid somebody to deliver the card to the top table, just as he was opening the cards with his second wife. Inside it read: "Deja vu – love Mummy and Daddy." Shirley knew nothing of this incident until he was told, and he was mortified. Afterwards, Paul did what Eunice's older daughters Linda and Carole had done, and he had nothing more to do with their mother.

The locals certainly thought Eunice was a character, another one who was the life and soul, but it is true to say that when she was drunk, she completely ruined family life. Nevertheless, Shirley never did leave her and deep down inside he probably didn't fancy the prospect of being on his own again. You have to remember that when she was on her game, Eunice did everything for him. Not only was she his manager, she cooked and cleaned and did everything else. Shirley was an old-fashioned kind of man who had the wife looking after the house, while he went out to work. He would have had trouble boiling an egg to be quite honest, but that was how things sometimes were back then.

Unlike Jim Royle from the hit TV show *The Royle Family*, Shirley always had a clean vest and pants, and he also grafted. He let Eunice deal with the finances and the house which was probably a mistake as he had no idea what was happening with the money. He wasn't one to invest it and keep an eye on the percentages they were making, and if he ever needed any cash all he did was ask Eunice and the cash would be there. His life was one of routines and systems, so he did not want to be tied up with paperwork and stuff like that.

Maybe the toughness of how things had been when he was a kid was what gave him the staying power in his relationship with Eunice, and he went on and married her knowing full well what she was like, but then again, almost anything is better than shutting that front door at the end of a day full of people and being totally and utterly alone. His first two marriages had failed, and after his second wife Sally had gone off the way she did it left a psychic injury of the mind and heart which would never completely heal. With Paul being that much older and off doing his own thing, and with his own children and stepchildren being wherever they were, the father and daughter bond he formed with Jane was the one thing that kept the both of them going. They were the best of mates, and they could deal with Eunice if they stood together.

As he got older Paul moved into the flat adjoined to the property, and he tended to keep out of the way until he eventually cut all of his ties after the wedding, which unfortunately meant Jane missed out on having her big brother about until they re-established contact for a short time in 2012, before Paul's untimely death in early 2013. Shirley did try ringing him up a little while before his death, and he did ask for Paul on his death bed, but the mental scars from Paul's childhood ran too deep and he didn't want to know.

It must have hurt Shirley having other children elsewhere in the world calling somebody else "dad". Unless you were downright evil you could not fail to be affected by such a situation no matter how many times you shrug your shoulders and say: "That's life." It doesn't matter if you're mixing with celebs, messing about with Tommy Cooper or Kim Wilde, or just standing on your jack at the end of Blackpool Pier looking out at the stormy sea and thinking back to that exact same spot so many summers before.

There had been so much pain that he had to laugh at it all, and take breathers. Maybe a swim at the Imperial Hotel in Blackpool, or a walk on the moors, all of this was necessary to stop him from going under. He had never set out to be a star, but stardom came calling. It wasn't about the money either; if he had a couple of quid in his pocket he was happy.

For everything he had, and all that he went on to achieve, Shirley would have traded it all in for peace, harmony and unrelenting love without any conditions. Rejection had been with all the Crabtree boys from an early age, and their father's departure was just the beginning. Shirley was somewhat reliable and safe, and this is how he dealt with life. Eunice, on the other hand, was a free spirit who once in drink didn't give a damn about anything or anyone. Jane would sit in her bed and wait for her dad to get home at night, praying that it would be soon, but of course, he could be anywhere in the country. The first thing he would do when he had put down his bag was go straight up to her room, and they enjoyed some fine moments together this way while Eunice was asleep.

There was many a time she came home from school and if her mother knew Shirley was away for a while she would go on the piss in the afternoon. Jane would very often find her asleep in the chair, and this is why Eunice's parents were a god-send. They came into the family home and looked after Jane, they were ashamed by the way their daughter behaved, and they had a lot of time and sympathy for Shirley.

Chapter Thirteen

On The Piss With Eunice

IF YOU were kitted out in your black leather jacket, and you had your collar up-turned, and if you were also wearing blue Levi jeans and Hush Puppies, you would have been well prepared for the 1950s revival which took place in the summer of 1978. Suddenly there was a new contender – the quiff was back to take on the afros, mohicans, and comb-overs adorning the dance floors of discothèques all over the country. From all of this, as we now know, the mullet evolved, but there were some of the craziest hairdos doing the rounds in the 1970s and the wearers really thought they looked cool.

It wasn't all Blondie and Dr Hook in 1978 though. There was also the Atari, the Electric Light Orchestra, the first test-tube baby, and of course, the hit movie *Grease*. Condoms could legally be purchased in Ireland for the very first time, which would not have interested lead actors John Travolta and Olivia Newton John because, as far as we know, they never did have a bunk-up in real life. With Travolta, and on her own, Newton John had massive hits, which were indeed good songs, although they tended to get on people's nerves after a while. Both actors were, however, smart enough not to sign up for the 1982 sequel *Grease 2*, which earned almost $660,000 less at the box office than video and DVD sales.

In England, at the time, the average cost of a house was around £16,000; a pint of beer cost 40p, and there were strikes all over the place with the public services. A Bulgarian defector called Georgi Markov was assassinated in a London street in September 1978 by a ricin-filled pellet which was shot from the tip of an umbrella like something straight out of a James Bond film.

The first Big Daddy match of the year happened on 7 January in Wolverhampton, when he teamed up with Honey Boy Zimba, against Haystacks and Hillbilly Hellon. After signing autographs and getting changed, Shirley would have probably got home around 12.30am if he didn't stop. The next evening he would have driven to Lincoln, then down south to Digbeth the night after that, before hitting Newark, Derby, Middlesbrough, Leicester, Keighley, Chester, Hanley, Cleethorpes, and Halifax with one day off in between. On 28 January, his tag match with Tony St Clair against Haystacks and Hillbilly Hellon was shown on TV, and it was the first one of the year for Shirley, who had really shone in front of the cameras in the run-up to Christmas 1977. He experienced a surge in popularity after he appeared at the Queen's Silver Jubilee celebrations at the Royal Albert Hall:

> *"For every wrestler and professional sportsman, there are special occasions that stand out in the memory for years afterwards. For footballers, it is walking out on to that pitch at Wembley Stadium to play in the FA Cup Final, or perhaps a major international, for cricketers they look back on matches against Australia at Lord's, and so it goes on. One of my delights was the royal occasion enjoyed by the whole of British wrestling in 1977 when HRH The Duke of Kent attended the Silver Jubilee Spectacular at the Royal Albert Hall. I've always been a patriotic type and proud to be British. Somewhere on my wrestling gear there is a Union Jack in every bout and for Jubilee year, I even had a special Union Jack design for my ring gown. Thus, I was especially pleased to be selected as one of the wrestlers to appear in that memorable program on Wednesday 30*

November 1977. Twice before the Duke of Edinburgh had attended gala wrestling bills at the Royal Albert Hall which included foreign as well as home-based wrestlers but this time, as befitted the occasion, it was an all-British line-up and as a result the Queen's Jubilee appeal funds were swelled by £10,000. I have never known a dressing room atmosphere like that night and every wrestler on the bill, plus the referees and officials of Dale and Martins Promotions, the matchmakers, paraded into the ring to be personally introduced to the Duke of Kent."

Business was booming for the Crabtrees and the ever-inventive Max was looking for bigger and better ways to use the Big Daddy character, which sometimes clashed with what Shirley wanted to do. There may have been disagreements but there was never really any falling-out between any of the brothers who kept business separate from family life. Just as the kids were not allowed into the dressing rooms or the ring, they were not allowed into the back room at Max's house. Brian lived on the end of the farm, and he would come up and they would all go off into the back to talk. Other times, Shirley would come up to the farm with Jane and, after stopping off at Brian's, his wife Sue would take the kids off with the horses, and Shirley would go on his own to Max's.

There was a debut for future British judo champion Chris Adams in 1978, and Irishman Dave "Fit" Finlay started wrestling in England for Joint Promotions, and then for Brian Dixon.

After seven years together, Shirley and Eunice finally tied the knot in Bromley, Kent, and as you can imagine Eunice did not stay sober. It was a small occasion with just the brothers and their wives in attendance, and then Shirley went off afterwards and wrestled. For better or for worse, they were together in the eyes of their maker now, and they would stay together until the end. Without Eunice, Shirley would not have been able to do what he did, but he certainly paid for it.

That is not to say Max didn't bear an influence as of course he did. He was the one who had the power to put his brother up there at the top of the bill against all the top wrestlers (or the ones who would wrestle him). A great deal of Shirley's publicity was done by him and Eunice without the help of any fancy public relations officers or spin doctors. The only thing that was spinning back then was Eunice's head the next morning if she had a heavy session on the sherry.

They may have been the brains behind the Big Daddy character, but Shirley was still on a £50-a-night wage, and Max pocketed a lot of money. Eunice found a lady called Jenny in Halifax who made Big Daddy teddy bears, and by selling these alongside posters and signed photos, they managed to make their money.

Jane had not known about her mum and dad's wedding and was shocked when she was told. It was done down south and kept quiet because Shirley didn't want the media to intrude. The newly-weds then went off on honeymoon on the *QE2* the following year when Shirley had some time in his schedule, but they did have a couple of days in Blackpool a few days later to celebrate. They would often go down there and have fish and chips; Shirley would always have two pieces of fish and a carton of mushy peas and once on the way home when Eunice attacked him while he was driving she got the whole pot right in the face.

Next she was screaming "stop the fucking car, I'll walk home" which Shirley would not do at first, and that was another nice family day out ruined. There was no way Eunice could walk back home to Halifax from Manchester, even if she was sober, so Shirley just carried on driving up the road beside her as she staggered along the kerb like a hooker covered in mushy peas. The poor families driving past them as Eunice was attacking Shirley must have wondered what was happening as the car swerved all over the road. All they would have seen was the driver trying to fend off his lunatic passenger; it wouldn't be until they drove up alongside that they would have got the shock of their lives when they realised that the driver was in fact Big Daddy.

The guy must have spent his whole life fighting, which wasn't a bad analogy at all. Peace and quiet were something other people had; it wasn't something which happened that often in any of the Crabtree households. If it wasn't Shirley and Eunice fighting it was Max and Eunice. On the night Shirley did Children in Need with Kim Wilde in 1983, Brian's wife Sue left him out of the blue and she never returned.

At times life did appear like one hard battle, and if the truth be told driving all around the country to throw yourself about when he should have been tucked up on the sofa with his tartan blanket was not the easiest way to earn a living. It was all Shirley had ever done; he knew nothing else, which didn't help when the time came for him to recognise that he had had enough. Those around him who were supposed to have loved him should have seen it too; Jane tried, but it fell on deaf ears. If Max and Eunice had made a plea, then it really could have happened. After wrestling, Shirley was like a lost sheep with no purpose. He was no good to Max anymore, and he was no use to Eunice, and he became only too aware of this.

Back in the day, those calmer occasions in Blackpool between Shirley and Eunice could be relaxing. He would go for a swim and a sauna while Eunice went and did some shopping. Afterwards, they would have some lunch, and then they would go back home. If Shirley wasn't outdoors in his paddling pool in the chilly evening air, he would be curled up with Jane under a tartan blanket drinking milky coffee. He loved his music and his films, and he had a big collection of both. He bought himself a top-of-the-range stereo, and they even bought one of those new fangled video recorders.

One time Shirley arrived home, and one of his favourite shows, *Mastermind,* was on. Eunice was answering every question correctly, and he thought she was absolutely amazing. He suddenly thought she had stopped being as daft as a brush and turned into a genius, and Jane didn't have the heart to tell him he was watching a recording that her mum had seen before. Shirley wasn't a technical person, and he didn't do much around the house, to be fair he was hardly ever home. On another occasion, Eunice dished up the most fantastic Yorkshire pudding and Shirley was amazed. Her terrible cooking skills were well known and, as he praised her up she made sure she hid the Aunt Bessie's packaging deep in the bin.

Every night, after the show, as Big Daddy he would experience the same thing. Hordes of people, mainly kids, waiting to see him, wanting to touch him, and he did his best to accommodate them all. He once told a reporter: "People give me more love than any human is entitled to", and he was genuinely appreciative of what they had made him.

For a while, it was really good, and the late 1970s and early 1980s were definitely the best time for Daddy in the ring. After 1982, there was a lot of re-hashing of old routines, and the truth is everybody had seen it done on so many occasions. At the same time, Big Daddy was at the peak of his fame, and his matches against Giant Haystacks were top of the pile. As the years rolled on he was made to look good by other wrestlers such as Tony St Clair and Banger Walsh who fought Shirley over 700 times. With the super charged atmosphere as well as the theatrics you really did come away from the shows having enjoyed yourself and there was truly a sense of the whole performance being greater than the sum of its parts.

The fact that Shirley was so popular, and he was so strong, meant he could get away with it but, if the tag wasn't right, the shows looked bad, and it got harder for him carrying the weight. Opponents had to be hand-picked so their style fitted in with Daddy's routine, or else it wouldn't work. At Joint, everyone was just a worker no matter how big a star. No one got any bonuses, and nobody except Shirley was allowed to sell their autographs and merchandise, and this pissed a lot of wrestlers off. If they were earning decent money there wouldn't have been the resentfulness but that was how it was. Every night they were paid by whichever of the Crabtree brothers was at the show. The wages would be brought down and dished out in little brown envelopes, and you got £6 per hundred miles travelling expenses, which was absolutely ridiculous.

In April 1978, Kendo Nagasaki appeared in the ring in a bizarre unmasking ceremony which was a bit of an anti-climax to be honest. The red contact lenses were pretty cool, and the shaven head was a nice touch, but the crowd were a little disappointed to find out that the great oriental master was, in fact, a chap called Peter from the Potteries. Drawing on the image of David Carradine's TV character Kung-Fu definitely wasn't one of Kendo's career highlights, and he retired for a while a few months later on doctors' orders and went into rock and roll management.

On FA Cup Final day, Shirley and Tony St Clair were up against Haystacks and Bruiser Moor, as Ipswich Town pulled off a shock result by beating Arsenal thanks to a goal from Roger Osborne.

Gradually, the mail pouring into the offices for Big Daddy started to become a problem. They did sift through it but were unable to reply to the vast majority. There was a lot of stuff which never reached Shirley, much of it didn't get any further than Max, but that was how it was. People offered him all manner of things, and there was a whole host of bizarre requests. Saying that, if Max saw something he thought was good he would pass it through to his brother.

In 1982, pioneering all-black friends of Africa magazine *New Envoy* wrote to Big Daddy asking him to be the guest of honour at the first black beauty queen contest, and you can almost see the thinking behind the approach. There was nobody bigger and whiter than the majority of their readership, and of course, he was a very patriotic-looking figure. The letter was penned by Patricia Thomas, the special events secretary, and it was certainly a forward-thinking gesture.

This was the early 1980s however, and attitudes toward race were very different to how they are today. Shirley never did go to the event, and it may have simply been a case of not having the time to do it. While a positive relationship could have been established between the black community and a national icon, there could have also been a backlash to what he was doing too. With 1981's Brixton riot fresh in people's minds a large portion of the white British public still felt like there was a "them and us" mentality between blacks and whites. Whatever the reasoning, Max would have seen it as a risk and Daddy's appearances would be more middle of the road and safe.

Another notable offer came from El Bandito himself. Orig Williams wrote to Shirley trying to arrange for Big Daddy to appear on television in Wales and Ireland which ITV would not have been happy with. Offering him £300 a match plus expenses the deal never came about, and it was a bold move on the Welshman's part.

Christmas was a lovely time to spend in the village of Millbank because of the close sense of community. There would always be something going on like a fête or a carol service at the church, and Shirley would usually get asked to come along. He would happily oblige if he was able to, and kids' faces would light up when they saw him appear. He would always be there to watch Jane in the nativity play, but of course, Christmas meant more opportunities to piss it up for Eunice.

When Shirley was home, and she had her serious head on, there was some sort of normality. There was a sense of magic and safeness surrounding her father, and Jane carried on believing in Father Christmas until around this time, when she learned the truth. Thinking she was asleep Shirley tiptoed into her bedroom with all of her presents, and that was the end of that. On Christmas Eve they would always go up to the farm and deliver presents, first to Brian's, and then to Max and Beryl's, and spend the evening there with their five boys. They had some good Christmases up at the farm, but in the end, it was spoiled by Eunice, who would have too much to drink, and Shirley put a stop to it in 1986.

Shirley, Eunice and the family would always open their presents at midnight, and by the time they came back down from the farm that year Eunice was very drunk indeed. She had bought Shirley a ghetto blaster, and all he did was make one comment about looking like a Jamaican with the machine perched on his shoulder, and Eunice thought he was taking the piss and stormed off and they ended up searching the village half of the night. Eunice's behaviour would make Shirley as mad as hell, but there were some occasions when she was downright evil as well as dangerous in drink, and this is why her children eventually blocked her out of their lives.

Around this time, there was an incident with the dog barking outside in the yard. Eunice decided to shoot at the poor thing with a .22 air rifle and Shirley went mental. His English bull terrier, Patch, was his pride and joy and was a spitting image of Bill Sykes's dog Bullseye from the film *Oliver Twist*.

When Shirley tried to stop her, it was then that she shot him and grazed the side of his head. There really were no lengths she would not stoop to; she even got drunk when she was babysitting years later. When Jane returned home, she said to Eunice: "Mum you've had a drink", and when she checked the babies' bottle she found that it was laced with vodka. After an argument, she slapped her mother across the face, and she left.

It wasn't until Jane moved out that she was able to finally have some peace and quiet, and Shirley would often come up for a cup of tea. The final thing she did before she left was pour a bottle of wine over her mother's head, and she told her if she liked to drink so much then she was going to give her one right then.

When she returned later that evening with Max's son Scott to pick up the rest of her stuff she noticed that Eunice was in a worse state than when she had left. She had injured herself, cutting her face and letting the blood drip down on to her clothes. When Jane walked in she looked at her dad but there was no need for her to explain herself. Shirley just laughed because he knew what Eunice was like.

Jane describes Shirley as her best friend, and they knew each other inside out and nothing needed to be said about Eunice's behaviour. Both agreed that if they didn't have each other, they would have no sanity in their lives at all. There was no way Shirley could have stopped Eunice from drinking even if he had wanted to because they spent so much time apart, and besides, she would hide it around the house. It wasn't that he was trapped in the relationship, but things happened to him that other men would not have put up with so there was definitely a certain amount of insecurity and nervousness in him. There were even times he couldn't face going wrestling and being up there in the ring for all of those people to look at. He was especially nervous in front of the TV cameras on a one-to-one, which would later become a problem when asked to make guest appearances, and the viewers did not always see the best of him in such situations.

When things were good, they were glorious. Maybe Shirley had just come back from a couple of weeks in the sun and the travelling schedule was not too strenuous for a week or so, and playing in front of packed houses certainly helped. There were a lot of good times.

There may have just been a general sense of contentment in Shirley if there had been no major bust-up with Eunice, and when things were this way life was sweet. You couldn't read a paper or a magazine in Britain at this time without at least a passing mention of Big Daddy whose fame was now established, although it was contained largely to home shores. A sober Eunice made things so much easier, she was a different animal, and she liked nothing more than to fuss over people. Shirley didn't need to lift a finger or make a cup of tea, and when there was a special occasion and she stayed away from the sauce they would have a brilliant time.

For one of the kid's birthday parties she put together a fantastic buffet and really pulled out all the stops. There was a sense of wanting to be needed in her, and the day after she had one of her drunken episodes she would be eating humble pie. There would be a bit of an atmosphere, and she would sheepishly carry on with her routine like nothing had happened even if she couldn't really remember what she had done. It was a weakness spurned from boredom; the booze was replacing something which was missing in her soul and perhaps letting a darker part of her personality show. The drink sent her into a fit of psychotic self-centred behaviour, and she really didn't care about anybody or anything.

As soon as she'd had a couple of mouthfuls of drink it went straight to her head, and you could hear it in her voice. You can imagine the flurry of nervous activity, which coursed through her when the producer of the TV series *This Is Your Life* telephoned one day and made an enquiry about doing a programme on Shirley. And of course, Eunice assured everyone that she would be able to keep her mouth shut no matter how pissed she was, and that Shirley wouldn't have a clue what was going on.

Chapter Fourteen

This Is Your Life

THE TRUTH is Shirley pretty much knew about *This Is Your Life* from the start. The family spent a large period of 1979 waiting for the show to happen, and he got more nervous the nearer they got to the date. Eunice had been on form one night and blurted something out, and the cover-up gave the game away.

Although Shirley never actually questioned her about it, he could see right through her, as he always could.

For Daddy, 1979 was all about the Mighty John Quinn, but Britain was in a state of crisis, although the Government was denying it. When Prime Minister James Callaghan returned from an international summit in early January to find the country in a state of industrial unrest, *The Sun* recorded his famous comment in the headline: "Crisis? What crisis?" This was the winter of discontent, and the axe was about to fall for the PM. In February, even the grave-diggers went on strike and as the bodies piled up in mortuaries all over the UK, Callaghan continued to talk through the vertical divide in his posterior.

Another body was found in a hotel room in New York City on 2 February. Sex Pistol Sid Vicious was found dead after choking on his own vomit after a suspected heroin overdose. He was on bail at the time for the second degree murder of his girlfriend Nancy Spugden the year before.

Another body leaving the continent around the same time was Canadian wrestler Quinn, although he was very much alive. Born in Ontario in Canada, when he first came to Britain to wrestle he stoked the fires by branding all Britons "cowardly". His first televised *World of Sport* fight was shown on 13 January and he knocked out Beau Jack Rowlands in Hemel Hampstead as a winning run began.

Despite warnings given in 1979 that too much showmanship would wreck wrestling, promoters continued to give the people what they wanted, and they weren't put off. Indeed, the viewing figures were good with ten million about average for a Saturday, but the prophecy had been made. Rather than a publicist driving what Daddy did, the media exposure happened because his character was genuinely adored by the papers and the public and these were his golden years. Later on, the tide did turn for Daddy with the papers, but when he first achieved fame there were few outside the wrestling world who resented what he was doing. You could argue that he was over saturated, but his age meant he wasn't going to be around forever. Something that amused Shirley when he first became famous was that other celebrities started to send him signed photographs.

On 4 May 1979, Margaret Thatcher took over from Callaghan as Prime Minister, and she was a fan of Big Daddy, so famously asked him for a signed photo. Quite often the Iron Lady would get her own way in cabinet meetings by holding opposing ministers in headlocks, or pinning them with the double elbow. The showdown between Daddy and Quinn came on FA Cup Final day, 12 May, and the build-up the weeks before saw him fight four of five televised contests. Quinn and Haystacks refused to appear in the final of a knockout contest in April, but he won all four of the other contests, three of them by knockout.

"It was in our own terrific newspaper Wrestling Scene that I first began to notice the name John Quinn. He obviously knew what the business was all about after

making his mark in North America and going via Japan and South Africa to a couple of years of good results in German tournaments. Even then I had no idea what he looked like and was able to get an impression of his ability only from the names of some of the opponents he had beaten. When I heard he was coming to Britain from the beginning of 1979 it didn't mean a great deal to me, other than the possibility that sooner or later I would find myself on the other side of the ring to a wrestling visitor to our country who had built quite an interesting reputation and deserved to be treated accordingly. Little did I realise how quickly that view would be shattered with Quinn becoming the most bitter rival of my entire wrestling career. He had hardly arrived in the country when he began shooting his mouth off and attacking British wrestling in general and Big Daddy in particular. Just why he decided to make me the main target of his attacks I never really discovered but as the weeks went by he became more and more cutting... Eventually it became clear the country wasn't big enough for the both of us and there was a solo showdown bout. Quinn had done a lot of shouting without backing his claims with action but he finally agreed to the bout which was included in wrestling's first big night at the 10,000 capacity Wembley Arena. Quinn came up with endless conditions for the contest – no rounds, no falls, last man standing to win, loser to quit British wrestling… and so it went on. I wasn't bothered. I told him I would be there and we would see who was the better man in the Wembley ring, conditions or no conditions."

Although Daddy had scored victories against Quinn as part of a tag team, the Wembley contest was to be their first singles match

176

but in truth, everyone knew it wouldn't last long. The televised bout on Cup Final day saw Daddy teamed up with Ringo Rigby, while Quinn was paired with Rollerball Rocco, but a singles match was a different kettle of fish for Shirley, who didn't wrestle solo very much by then. Coming to the ring to the familiar sound of 'We Shall Not Be Moved', Shirley had finished with the Union Jack gown he had worn in the Jubilee year. Instead, he donned the Jamaican-coloured gold, green, and black so it is possible getting the ghetto blaster had a subconscious effect, although he had not the slightest resemblance to Bob Marley or any of the Rastafarians.

Maybe it was the bang to the head he had received when he did the real fighting at home with the wife. The little darling had clonked him one with a baseball bat a few months back, and he looked a right state for a while. Forever he was caught between the devil and the deep blue sea. On a good day, Eunice was a big influence, employing Margaret Mansfield to make his sequin capes and hats, and she had a great head for business. She also got a machinist in the village to put together Big Daddy teddy bears, and they tried a few different merchandising ideas to try to make people feel like they were a little nearer to him.

> *"The big night was Wednesday 27 June 1979, and it is an occasion I will never forget. The atmosphere as I walked into the ring with my brother Brian as a special second was incredible and it seemed like absolutely everyone in this capacity crowd was willing me to win. I had trained and prepared for this bout like none before and was feeling on top of the world. I expected Quinn to try and force the pace and he did just that and I took some heavy blows. Then, not content with slamming me he attacked Brian and I really saw red. That was the ultimate spur and after a series of slams I took him over the top with a reverse double elbow lift and backdrop and Quinn didn't move again until*

*revived by the ambulance men in the back room some
12 minutes later. Next day he left Britain."*

It was indeed one of Shirley biggest performances as Big Daddy
and, and if you had blinked you would have missed it. The
atmosphere was absolutely electric and there was a real dislike
for the bearded Canadian, who had stood there in the ring in his
green leotard and taunted the crowd.

Shirley's daughter Jane was ten years old at the time and could
not believe the atmosphere. The place was packed to the rafters
and it felt like a big rock concert, and she can remember looking
up at Shirley beneath the lights in the middle of the ring and
thinking: "Wow; that's my dad." Unsurprisingly, it wasn't the
action in the ring that she remembers most from that remarkable
night; she can recall looking at the crowd and seeing everybody
happy, and that was brilliant.

They were all completely immersed in the spectacle before
them, and you would have been hard pushed to find one person
who was not smiling. Halfway through the two minutes the
bout actually lasted, Quinn had his pop at Brian Crabtree, and it
ignited the crowd further. Then, for around a minute after this, it
got about as lively as it would ever get for Big Daddy as a wrestler
as he finished off Quinn.

Because of Shirley's involvement with shows like *Tiswas*, as
well as the wrestling, it got to the stage where he knew influential
people in television, and they would ring him up direct to ask him
to do appearances so the ones in the know had to make sure they
did not let on to him about *This Is Your Life*. Eunice told the kids
what was happening and got them to promise not to tell their dad
what was happening, and then she went and spoiled the surprised
before they had a chance. The hints she dropped were not subtle
and Shirley was not daft.

On the day, they took the train down to London where they
were met by the BBC driver who took them to the theatre. They
were all seated around a great big round table; Jack Wilkinson was

there, and they all went through the script to make sure everybody knew what they had to say and when Eamonn Andrews sprung the trap Shirley was genuinely surprised. Like a rabbit caught between the headlights, he was not naturally comfortable with the spotlight on him, but he was also thinking: "Oh shit, what are they going to be dragging out of the woodwork?"

It was the personal nature of certain types of programme which Shirley didn't like and that is why he would never do shows like *Parkinson*. When it was all over the look of relief he had in his eyes was there for all to see, and he just wanted to go home and curl up into one great big ball so the world could not get in. The demand and pursuit of his time was relentless; it was only when he was back home in Millbank that he could have a normal life, and this lack of freedom was the downside to what he achieved.

When everybody finally settled down and took their seats on the stage, Eamonn began his commentary and Shirley began to relax a little more. He was not as relaxed as Eamonn, who had been out the back drinking brandy with Eunice before the show, so he was certainly ready to go. They would continue their merriment afterwards with Eunice putting on all the airs and graces; she was actually putting on a posh voice and the kids were trying not to laugh. The facade would fall down as soon as she was hammered, but before that she was charming, walking around like she was Lady Muck or Cleopatra more like.

The BBC make-up artist had done her up so she looked like an Egyptian, whereas she usually wouldn't wear any make-up at all. There was a moment on stage when Jane suddenly realised that her mother had been on the drink, and Shirley realised the same thing at about the same time. Then, there was a moment of mutual panic as they wondered exactly what she might do or say, but the show passed without incident. When Anita Harris came on screen and talked about Shirley helping teach her how to weight train, Eunice was not very happy at all, and that is as close as they got to trouble. Shirley obviously hadn't told his wife about his meeting with the beautiful young ice skater and actress, and if you watch the show you can actually see his reaction to the situation.

When his colleague from the Coldstream Guards came bounding in Shirley was lost for words, but carried on even so. The truth was he had no clue who the guy was; he could have been Lord Lucan as far as he was concerned, but he shook his hand all the same. When it was all over he had no desire to hang around and watch Eunice getting drunk with Eamonn, so he and Max had it away on their toes while Shirley was still numb with shock. Jane was sat quietly in the corner with Haystacks, and being ignored by all of them when he suddenly turned to her and said: "Don't worry; nobody likes me either."

As the party went on Eunice had a blazing row with Brian, before she told Jane how disappointed she was in her as a daughter. After this, she tried to mess up Mick McManus's hair, and when Shirley later found out what had gone on he was glad that he had left when he did.

It wasn't that he did not feel honoured by *This Is Your Life,* he always recalled the day with great fondness, and saw it as one of the best days of his life. Sometimes it did all get on top of him though, and it felt like at any time he may suddenly wake up from a dream, or that the crowd would find him out. Like he was a phoney, an imposter living inside such a hulking frame, and if this happened there would be no Shirley Crabtree. His image soared high above what he was as a mere man, and in the back of his mind he knew that one day it would all come crashing down around his ears. He did his best to enjoy his here and now fame, and was always aware that it would end. And as the 1980s moved on and he got older, it grew harder to keep up the pretence.

"*Many of you have wondered what the reaction would be if you were suddenly confronted by Eamonn Andrews, carrying that famous read book and uttering those immortal words. Well, now I know, and the impact is shattering. I was cornered by Eamonn after wrestling at Croydon's Fairfield Halls, and I can honestly say I hadn't a clue it was coming. They told me afterwards that almost a year of planning went into the programme and chief plotters were my wife Eunice and brother Max and Thames Television researcher Maurice Leonard... I enjoyed every second of the recording which took place the next day. The whole thing was done in a really relaxed way and the first to greet me was Anita Harris the singing star who I helped to learn weight training at Crystal Palace. Then after more than 20 years I was reunited with Jack Wilkinson whom I played rugby with in Halifax as a schoolboy before Jack went on to represent England at rugby league. Next came my very first wrestling opponent Sandy Orford, and later Mick McManus, who gave me some very amusing personal reminiscences about what it was like to be on the receiving end of my belly-butt. From my time in the guards came a fellow Coldstreamer called Robert Robinson and an old friend from my lifeguard days in Blackpool, Hamilton Smith, now a top international swimming coach. I was introduced to people I had rescued at Blackpool and not seen since those days, among them a lady called Barbara Burkett. Then, there was a special welcome from Kerry Frogatt, a girl from Derbyshire whose parents were kind enough to say that I helped in her recovery from a brain tumour. Kerry was ten at the time and when her mother wrote asking for a picture I sent her some flowers and chocolate too, and we have kept in touch with them ever since."*

More contests against John Quinn were to come in the new decade, but none caught the imagination and the crowd like the Wembley bout in 1979, even if the end product was a disgrace. Things were so hectic that year; there wasn't even time for a summer holiday, although they did manage a few days away in the New Year. When Shirley turned up at Lourdes in south-west France, a major place for Roman Catholic pilgrimages, he was greeted with open arms. Famously, Lourdes has been the place visited in search of a miracle, and they certainly got one that day.

Some people were even wheeled up in beds, and you can imagine their faces when they saw Big Daddy. They were far from shocked when they looked up from being bathed in the restorative grotto spring water, and one of the religious people there told Shirley that he had done more to lift their morale than he could have possibly known.

As the 1980s grew ever closer, and Shirley marked his 49th birthday in November, he showed no signs of slowing down, and he rarely had more than a day or two off during that period of time. Surprisingly, he did not feature in the TV wrestling over the Christmas period; his last one in front of the cameras that decade was a tag match with Mal Kirk at the end of November in Leicester. They fought Haystacks and Rocco as a technician strike started to affect programming. The last fight of the year for Shirley was with Steve Grey against The Bulk and Sid Cooper a couple of days before Christmas, and Shirley was lucky enough to get a couple of weeks off during the holiday.

Around this time, the government announced a plan for council tenants to buy their own houses, which of course raised the vital cash they needed to get themselves out of trouble and kick-start the economy. With a lot of the major stars of British wrestling getting older, the business was perhaps waning a little, although the TV people wouldn't agree. It just started to feel like the whole industry was not moving with the times, although you wouldn't have turned around and called it old hat just yet.

With Daddy, McManus, and other top names, they were still able to pack out halls and stadiums, but it is true to say the golden age of the British game was coming to the start of its final furlong. Within five years the empire would really start to crumble but until then there was still time for Shirley to enjoy life as a top sports star on home shores and the amount of mail and offers he had at this time was truly staggering.

Opportunities were coming out of the woodwork, and they tried as best they could to organise shows around Shirley's other appearances. If he had enough notice, they could plan his schedule, but it did not always work out like that.

Another honour bestowed upon him around this time was that of the biggest chest in Britain. It was measured at 64in and was an official Guinness record at the time, so it was all good publicity. In the space of three years Big Daddy had come a long way. After dropping the bad-guy act it really had been a rollercoaster ride to success which ended up with appearances in the most prestigious places, meeting royalty and celebrities from all across the world.

One day while he was training in his gym, which was right in the middle of Sowerby Bridge with its steep hills, cobbles, and grey stone buildings, there came a knock at the door. Shirley didn't hear it at first as he was working out on the heavy bag, but when he shouted to whoever it was to come in and got no response he went to investigate. Outside a small crowd had gathered in the street to watch the man getting out of the posh car, which had bumped up on to the kerb and parked. Even the traffic warden put away his notepad and pen, and when he opened the door thinking it was going to be a couple of Jehovah's Witnesses trying to give him a copy of the *Watch Tower* he was surprised to see Prince Charles standing there.

Although Shirley invited the heir to the throne in for a brew, Charlie had it away on his toes. He told Shirley that he was just passing through, and that he just wanted to meet him and that was that. There was no in-depth conversation about quantum mechanics, black holes, or the new Ford Cortina, and Shirley didn't say: "Give my love to your mum." The two men just stood there smiling at each other for a few seconds as women wearing tabards, with curlers in their hair, stood on their doorsteps and watched.

There was of course no social media back then, and if you had a camera you were doing well. Such a meeting today would be all over the Internet in minutes but back then it just stood as it was. Somebody had pointed out that Daddy's gym was up ahead, and that was enough for the Prince. He said something like: "Big Daddy, one has always wanted to meet one", they had a brief conversation, and then the Prince departed and Shirley shut the door and chuckled to himself under his breath. Who would have believed it?

Chapter Fifteen

We Shall Not Be Moved

W ITH THE 1980s beginning and the Big Daddy phenomenon in full swing the time was right for him to
exploit his image to the maximum and that is what he did.
At the start of the decade, the global positioning system time
epoch began, and the Winter Olympics started in Lake Placid,
New York. Back at home, in a bid to stop people from striking,
Margaret Thatcher announced that state benefits would be halved
to those on the picket line which made people mad. The big hits
early on were The Jam's 'Going Underground' (in celebration
of the grave-diggers' 14 per cent pay rise perhaps?), 'Geno' by
Dexy's Midnight Runners, and The Vapors' 'Turning Japanese'.

Suddenly, Britain's finest pop stars had some competition, as
a single released by Big Daddy and the Titanic Survivors began
to appear. It had been made by Shirley's old friend from the club
days, Lonnie Cook, who noticed the copies they had of 'We Shall
Not Be Moved' by The Seekers were starting to sound very crackly
indeed, and finding other copies was becoming impossible. He
put the suggestion to Shirley that they should record it themselves,
and he also managed to convince a friend who was a local EMI
rep.

Suddenly, Bob Barratt (one of their house producers) was in
touch with Lonnie about the project and when Bob went to talk to
Lonnie, he sold him the idea. They were booked in at the Olympic

studios in London and Lonnie recalls that Shirley found the recording studio a very daunting place, and he exhibited the signs of nervousness he experienced doing TV shows.

Despite the nerves, Shirley did shows like *Tiswas* in the early 1980s because he knew it was a natural progression for somebody who was largely a children's entertainer, but he turned down more adult shows such as *Parkinson* and *Wogan* where the questions were perhaps a little more testing than how many pies he ate, and who his best match was against. And talking of pies, the custard one he got in the face in November 1980 nearly choked him while Haystacks sat there pissing himself.

Shirley did what was necessary but didn't necessarily enjoy that kind of work, which was a shame because he certainly was a presence before the cameras, and this is why both his music and television presenting careers were so brief. Like some great uncle, the kids loved him, and in Leicester in December he turned up dressed as Santa where a fantastic series of pictures were taken before he teamed up with Kid Chocolate in the ring to overcome Banger Walsh and Butcher Bond.

Despite the nerves, some of the stuff Shirley did on *Tiswas* was pretty good, and he did appear regularly. Perhaps his best was an interview with Sally James with kids sitting all around. You can really feel his presence beneath the cameras as he sits casually talking about his life, after giving away a giant Big Daddy teddy bear, and you can see how some producer somewhere would have looked at that and thought him capable of hosting his own show.

After the interview with Sally, one of Daddy's most hilarious TV moments occurred, and it was one of those times when what was supposed to happen just didn't come off and there were side splitting repercussions, apart from the bloke breaking his leg. A tiny man half of Shirley's size appeared centre stage dressed as a Roman centurion. More reminiscent of Hengist Pod from *Carry On Cleo* than Russell Crowe's *Gladiator,* he came out with the quote: "Now is the winter of my discontent", and his concerned smile suggested that he really was in trouble.

Nevertheless, presenter Chris Tarrant pushed on like a true professional, and told the audience that the bloke was probably the world's strongest human, and that he could lift any two men in Great Britain. Just then Shirley emerged from the left sporting an orange sports vest and blue tracksuit bottoms, wiping away custard from around his neck.

Bernard Manning (who was allowed on TV back then) emerged from the right in a state of disbelief as the camera panned out to reveal a scaffold pole with a chain seat on either end. When the man placed the bar on his shoulders behind a protective strap, Bernard's one-liners reduced the sketch into a farce. None too concerned to regain control, Chris Tarrant just let it go as Shirley boomed with laughter as Bernard came out with quips like "you can do it son", "how about a song first", and "this act is worth more in scrap". Then the two big men stared down at the shorter man in disbelief and the stunt began.

Predictably, it ended in misery, and after trying to balance the two men on either end of the pole all three crashed to the floor in fits of laughter. Then they went again, on the promise that this time they would get it right, and once again they crashed to the floor in what must surely be regarded as a television comedy gem. For a second, the bloke did actually hold Daddy's weight, and we saw him swinging about in the air on the chain seat before dropping to the ground as Bernard got on and tipped the balance.

For the single, EMI drove Shirley and Lonnie down to London to do the recording, and they also laid on champagne and a fancy buffet which neither of them touched because they didn't drink and Shirley just ate massive salads in the day. At the end of the company working day, EMI arranged for all of their staff to come down to the studio for the chorus to give the effect of a big crowd for the final singalong. Arranged by Colin Fretcher, they did well to finish the record in one day considering there was a brass section, a wrestling timekeeper with a bell doing a voice-over, and of course, all of the photographs they took for the cover and publicity shots.

The single was released in April 1980, and was sold primarily at the wrestling which was a shame because it shifted so many copies that if it was sold in chart record shops it would have made the top 40. The name "Titanic Survivors" was thought up by Bob Barrett because he felt "Big Daddy" alone was not catchy enough. With Lonnie coming from Stoke-on-Trent, the same place as the captain of the *Titanic*, Edward Smith, Bob dreamed up the name.

> *"They wanted me to make others records, but I don't think I've had a more harrowing day than the one I had in the studio just doing the two sides. I started at 10am, and we worked until 2am, the following day. I couldn't go through that again, you have to be cut out for that sort of work. They do the instrumental first, then the vocal backing, and the singer last of all.*
>
> *"I was surprised at how popular the song was, and watching people like Elvis, or John Lennon and the Beatles on the telly; they used to make it all look so easy, but nothing in the studio is easy if you ask me. Other folks are naturals; they are not fazed at all in the studio or in front of the camera; one of my favourite actors was funnyman Tony Hancock, who made it look ever so simple... Acting out a part on the telly, or having a personal interview, is very different to wrestling on TV, it is a different sort of adrenaline that gets your heart racing. In the ring, you're thinking about your opponent, really zoning in on them, and you can be quite unaware of the audience. Doing TV, or recording a record in the studio, is an absolute nightmare, and is not something I could do every week. Imagine what an album for the kiddies would have been like if I'd have done that, I'd have pulled my hair out."*

During 1980, Shirley made just seven appearances on television in wrestling matches, but this did not mean his schedule had eased up. It was just the opposite, although he was still putting in the miles and going all over the country. On top of that he was doing a whole host of other things, including guest appearances or visiting sick children in hospital, as well as photo-shoots and recordings.

We have talked about Daddy being overexposed, but it is interesting to discover that he wasn't wrestling on TV almost every week like some have suggested. It was simply everything else he did outside the ring that gave people the impression that he wrestled on TV so much. One of his biggest matches of the year wasn't televised at all, but he fought in front of another packed house at Wembley that summer. He teamed up with Wayne Bridges, and they beat none other than The Mighty John Quinn and a fighter called Yasu Fuji.

It didn't matter who they were up against though, the money was just the same, although you got a bit more for a TV performance. There were other more sinister ways to earn a few extra quid too.

The outcome of a fight was usually known of course, but if the crowd took to the man booked to lose the result could change. If a contest went flat, and it needed a bit of something to lift it up again the promoters would sometimes demand blood. Max would tell a fighter to cut themselves on the face with a razor and for doing that they would get an extra fiver in their wages, but as Daddy, Shirley was never asked to do it because of all the children who used to watch him.

Despite the limitations of his performances, people got worked up and when it all came together it really was entertaining. It wasn't just his brothers who thought he had something special; when he appeared at the fundraising gala at the London Palladium in 1980, he was instantly recognised by Princess Margaret. After the show, she told him when he walked on stage the audience could feel his presence, which was very flattering indeed. Brian recalls it had always been this way with Shirley, even before he was famous. People would turn their heads and look at him as he walked by even when he was a 14-year-old boy.

To celebrate 25 years of televised wrestling Shirley appeared on the front of *TV Times* (dated 22 November 1980) in a white leotard, with Kent Walton slung over his shoulder holding on for dear life. The caption read: "Kent Walton's ringside view on 25 years of TV wrestling", but there was another caption at the top of the page which talked about the "king of the ring" eating 100 meat pies a week which was absolutely ridiculous.

For a couple of weeks, the magazine printed Shirley's life story, and there were lots of pictures taken up at the farm with the brothers, wives and children. It all looked very much like a scene out of *The Waltons* as they played happy families, their rural lifestyle looking idyllic, and they took pictures of Shirley looking like the country gentleman with walking stick and dog. They snapped another shot of the brothers at the stables with their arms around one other and Brian's horses in the background, and everything was hunky-dory. There were no major dramas on the day which pleased the brothers very much, and some decent photos were taken. Everybody was on their best behaviour because this was work, and for once the wives and kids were involved. If anybody messed up, or Eunice had been anywhere near the drink, there would have been hell to pay.

Chances are she still had a nip or two, but she was very crafty with where she hid the bottles. Of an evening, she would bring in a milky coffee for Shirley as he sat there watching the TV with Jane, who would take one look at her mother and know she was secretly having a drink out in the kitchen. She would whisper to her not to tell her dad, and that was the cat-and-mouse game she played. Rather than be open and honest about having a drink or two she would hide it in the oven or in the tumble-drier and places like that. It was this secretive behaviour that used to make Shirley angry.

Soon he was endorsing more and more things, and if there was paperwork to be signed, he wouldn't question it. He would usually sign without looking. Why would he need to? They were all brothers working together, right? Whether or not everything was always down the line is unknown but there were occasions when there were discrepancies.

Mistakes can be made but something that happened later in Shirley's life angered him a lot. They were driving down Queens Road in Halifax and they saw an advertisement for a newly-launched alcoholic drink, and there was Big Daddy on the advertisement. When he rang Max he was as mad as hell seeing as he was teetotal, and there he was advertising an alcoholic drink, and of course, he had not given his permission. As far as the families were concerned as soon as Shirley stepped out of the ring nobody had any holds over him, but this was not always the case. Max said he had simply "forgotten" to tell him about the deal, and when he gave Shirley his cut he went out and bought a new car with the money. Why the hell he bought a Lada we will never know, but by then the fortunes were depleting.

He did not have the pulling power in the 1990s that he once had. In 1984, he had become the face of Daddies Sauce for a while which helped to shift a few bottles, and his image was on everything. There was even a *Big Daddy Joke Book* in 1981, which was published by Armada Books, and Shirley did a few book signings to endorse it. On the back, it said: "Laugh, or else!" and it did well as a Christmas stocking-filler. Like many of the products he put his name to, he had very little to do with its content. His was simply a name which was popular, and it could be used to sell almost anything.

Saturday 20 June is a date that would remain in Shirley's head because that is the day his fight against Giant Haystacks at Wembley Arena was shown and 18 million viewers tuned in. There are all sorts of statistics comparing the size of this audience proportionally to the audiences for American wrestling at its peak, and that night blows everything out of the water.

The nation watched on as Daddy came to the ring with his friend Reverend Mike Brooks, who had of course wrestled himself. Once again, the atmosphere was electric, like so many of his performances back then, and the Arena was packed. The fact that the fight lasted for less than two and a half minutes before Haystacks disappeared over the top rope and into the table below was not exactly value for money, and if you were out making a cup of tea in preparation for the fight you may well have missed it. If you had paid money to see it, you may just have felt you were hard done by but the public interest in Big Daddy, and British wrestling in general, was still there.

The truth is Shirley was really pushing mentally and physically, but he had certainly had longer and better fights. He had just about got away with the John Quinn fight a couple of years previously, and there were other exciting matches to come, but the question was starting to be asked just how long the Big Daddy bandwagon would continue before people had had enough.

There was another tragedy in 1981, when Mike Marino died. Shirley had fought him many times, and his death was a big loss to the whole of the wrestling world. Apparently, while returning home to South London from a tournament in Folkestone, he had some kind of convulsive attack while driving on the M20, and he died by the roadside.

Chapter Sixteen

The Chip-Fat, Kiss-Me-Quick Hat World Of British Wrestling

DESPITE ALL of this life in the village continued pretty normally. There would be periods when it wasn't good but that would always run its course, and the decent would kick back in for a time. For the kids at school there may have been the occasional jibe about their father and Jane got a bit of bullying, but it was nothing major. Although she did not need to work she got herself a Saturday job in 1981, aged 12. The independence it gave her helped her to stand on her own two feet, and the lessons Shirley taught her about life have served her well over the years.

Paul, being that much older, was not influenced to such an extent because he was off doing his own thing. With her first wage, Jane bought Shirley a pair of blue leather boxing gloves, which were ever so slightly too small for his hands. Nevertheless, he would always train in his gym with the gloves simply because she had bought them for him. There was never a reluctance to train as it was something that he did naturally every day. Perhaps towards the end of his wrestling career it started to get a bit too much. In the end, after years of telling him and pleading with him to stop Jane would finally convince her father to call it a day, but when the TV slipped away in 1988, he was 58 years old and the necessity to go on the road became even greater. It must have been with much personal pain and anguish that Shirley continued to push himself although, of course, you would have never noticed.

A 16-year-old called Robbie Brookdale was making his debut in 1982 for Brian Dixon and Bobby Barron, and it did not take him long to hit the TV screens in both singles and tag contests. There was also a cartoon caricature of Big Daddy doing the rounds, and this was another avenue they could exploit. Barrie Tomlinson was the editor of *Tiger* and *Roy of the Rovers* at the time, and they were always using celebrities in their stories. They had used people like Geoff Boycott and Suzanne Dando, and then of course Big Daddy.

This eventually led to the commissioning of a Big Daddy annual which was published in 1983, and the very fact that they did another the following year means it must have sold well. They published lots of one-off celebrity annuals but very few did a second year, and they did well to tap into the success they had achieved with Big Daddy in the comics. In the *Tiger*, Daddy met Johnny Cougar which Barrie used to write, and he enjoyed bringing cartoon Daddy to life. And what was the outcome of the contest between the two great cartoon characters? A draw of course. Barrie also remembers trying to get some action shots of Daddy and Haystacks crashing together and very nearly getting crushed himself as the two men fell to the canvas nearby.

When *The Eagle* was relaunched in 1982, Barrie asked Shirley to be the guest star, and he turned up as Big Daddy clutching the very first copies of the comic. The event happened at the Waldorf Hotel in London and as the Royal Artillery Trumpeters played a fanfare, Daddy crashed through a screen before sitting on the bonnet of a mini-van reading the comic. It was great publicity and really helped get things going for *The Eagle* which continued for another 12 years, and he was also drawn by Mike Lacey for *Buster*.

Around this time, Shirley and Eunice were invited to Sandown races for a posh event, and of course the wife got so drunk on champagne that she started verbally abusing Gareth Hunt who was starring in the Nescafé adverts at the time. She told him he could grind her coffee beans any time he wanted, before she directed a swear word at him which rhymed very closely with his surname.

After watching Shirley on *Tiswas*, the bosses at ITV decided that *The Big Daddy Saturday Show* was going to replace it, and of course, the money they were offering was something Shirley didn't want to dismiss. It is a shame it never happened because the show may well have extended Shirley's run and made it possible for him to move away from the ring.

This would have favoured almost everybody. Shirley would not have had to drag his arse around and risk breaking his neck for money so late in his life, and the other wrestlers would have got their profession back. Only Max would have been left out in the cold, but he was a survivor and he would have soon whipped another wrestler into shape to fill the considerable gap left by his brother. In fact, it may have taken a couple of wrestlers such was the draw of Big Daddy back then, but for whatever reason it never came about.

The TV station even got as far as putting together a pilot and the opening credits had to be hastily edited when the show launched as simply *The Saturday Show* in October 1982. The official reason for Shirley backing out was on doctor's orders, but in truth there were a few reasons.

Not only would it have been one hell of a commitment and meant him reducing his wrestling appearances, Shirley really did feel like a fish out of water. When he got going he was fantastic in front of the cameras, but there were times when he just wanted the earth to swallow him up. Due to star with Isla St Clair, who said working with Daddy would be quite a bit different to working with Larry Grayson, in the end he pulled out and there never were any financial implications, or legal action about the broken contract.

It would have been difficult for the spotlight to have been on Shirley as a presenter of a Saturday morning children's TV show and it really wasn't his intention to pull out of the programme at the last moment. Gradually, he realised this kind of job wasn't for him, and his flamboyance didn't come out like it did during one-off interviews or at the wrestling. The show was hastily re-branded, and Tommy Boyd was brought in to co-host with Isla St Clair. It was then that Shirley realised that he would have to continue to wrestle if he wanted to earn a wage.

"My ambition is to keep happy and to make other people happy. Every second of every minute of every day I'm shaking hands, signing autographs and saying 'hello'. I'm told I look like the Pied Piper of Hamelin.

"It is the simple things in life that do it for me. Some people who are well known, famous if you like, they want to be in the limelight all the time even when they say they don't want it. They kind of need it, tend to thrive on it but that's not me at all. I'm happy to please myself, go for a walk on the moors with the dog, or relax at home and watch a good film. I don't need or want the glare of the media around me; I save that for when I'm Daddy the wrestler and famous personality. As I've said before, the people have made me, for some reason, they took me to their hearts and for that I am truly grateful.

"It hasn't been the easiest of lives to live, but I've done alright. I've tried to get a bit of enjoyment out of every day. I tried not to look too deeply into things and analyse it all because that sends you around the twist. I just do what I do because it is all I know, and of course, I love wrestling. I keep my life simple. I'm lucky enough to earn my living doing something I love, and I have a fantastic family… Sometimes you don't want

to be bothered, but most times people who stop you just want to be good-natured.

"Nevertheless once I gave up the business I did try to do things, so I wouldn't be noticed so much. I did try to get Shirley Crabtree back with different colour hair styles, hats, and stuff like that."

Despite the intense glare of the media spotlight being constantly on him, Shirley did his best to be professional at all times, and of course, he expected those around him to do the same. It was the press who made him a massive star and they also had the power to break him in half.

Shirley took it all incredibly seriously and one of the things he couldn't get over was the emotions, a mix of anger and amazement that spectators showed in their faces, and one of Jane's early memories was witnessing the effect her father had on people when he entered the ring. It was like Clark Kent taking off his glasses and unbuttoning his shirt, or Doctor Who stepping out of his TARDIS.

When he raised his sequined hat high in the air and started chanting "Easy! Easy! Easy!" he was totally hypnotic. And of course live wrestling was the highlight of so many people's week or month whenever there was a show in town. Shirley loved nothing more than working up the crowd and Jane can remember one ring entrance she made with her father as part of his entourage in particular. She had their bulldog Benson on a lead when a little boy put his hands through the ropes to stroke the dog. Jane said "get off my dog" and received one hell of a bollocking from her dad. He told her that it was not a professional thing to do and that the TV station had to cut it out of their recording, which had of course cost time and money.

As a father Shirley could be strict, but he also had a lot of love to give, and he never raised a hand to Jane. He used to say "you can hurt more with words than you can with action" and of course, he was right. In 1983, he appeared alongside Kim Wilde on Children in Need and helped them to raise money, and this was the sort of television he was best at.

The image of Big Daddy as the all-powerful, all-conquering hero was something nobody could live up to, and it was a strain for him at times although he did enjoy it. When you are appearing on television, in comics, and on records, it is very easy for the character you are portraying to become detached from the real person. Shirley was fortunate to have seen people rise and fall a long time before him. He knew only too well that nothing lasted forever but this wouldn't make letting go any easier when the time came.

On FA Cup Final day in 1983, Brighton & Hove Albion shocked their more famous opponents Manchester United by drawing with them 2-2 at Wembley. The wrestling afterwards saw Daddy teaming up with Kid Chocolate against a pair known as the Masked Marauders, and of course, they were defeated by knockout. The wrestling bout had been taped; live performances were usually kept for paying customers. This was, however, the beginning of the death throes for Big Daddy and British wrestling, although he let himself continue for a good few years afterwards.

In 1986, network TV introduced American wrestling to the masses, and suddenly everything was bigger and better and British wrestling couldn't compete. It was the wrong time of life for Shirley to be doing what he was doing but continue he did.

By the mid-1980s, it wasn't really the wrestling that people wanted him for; he became a phenomenon in his own right, appearing on shows such as *Surprise, Surprise* with Cilla Black, *That's Life*, and *Cannon and Ball*. Wrestler Ray Robinson (who made his first television appearances in the early 1980s) remembers a time when they walked into a hall full of small children, and when they saw Daddy, the place fell silent and Shirley made a remark about feeling like he was part of the *Sooty Show*. The night before, he had the same effect on a largely Asian community in Bradford. Once he had that microphone in his hand, he had everybody's undivided attention no matter their colour, creed, or age. His fame at this time meant that Big Daddy was much bigger than the wrestling gimmick he had started out as.

The Saturday Show would have meant a lot of things to a lot of people, and other wrestlers such as Giant Haystacks, Mick McManus, and Banger Walsh would have also got in on the act. The opening credits (which had to be hastily re-edited) cost thousands of pounds and started with cartoon Daddy belly-butting people across the screen. Banger's role every week would have been to accompany the guest star (people like Christopher Reeve or Adam West) or whoever was big on *Top of the Pops* at the time. For the pilot, they recorded a scene with Nicholas Hammond, who was portraying Spiderman on TV, and he had also played Friedrich Von Trapp in *The Sound of Music*. Nicholas came on, and he and Banger had a row and it all looked really good until four days later when he heard the show had been pulled.

There were a couple of things that happened around this time which really pissed Banger off, and it started with the death of his sister. One night Shirley dropped him on his knee during a fight and it broke. He didn't mean to do it; it was just one of the things that sometimes happened, an occupational hazard so to speak. What made it worse was if he didn't work, then he did not get paid. He had to top up the low wages he got wrestling by driving lorries so all of these things were going through his head as he lay in his hospital bed.

It was then that he received the news that his kid sister had been killed in a car crash, and that sent him over the edge. Add to this that none of the Crabtrees visited or even sent a card, let alone turned up at the funeral, and it suddenly dawned on Banger the true nature of his relationship with them. The only call he got was from Max, who asked when he was coming back to work, and that was that. Because they probably couldn't have all come down to see him, or turned up at the funeral, it wouldn't have hurt for one of them to have made the time and seen Banger was OK for a few quid, but it did not happen. A simple bouquet of flowers may have even done the trick.

Banger was one of the people who did the necessary donkey work which kept Shirley up on top, and he knew Max wouldn't let anybody topple him. This was the nature of the business, and when young wrestlers came in it took them a while to realise this. They were never going to destroy the empire no matter how skilful and flamboyant they were, and this is the thing those who didn't like the Crabtree brothers held against them.

It was all starting to become a little unbelievable in the ring with Daddy, and his sideways move into television and other mediums may well have prolonged the business and given it a chance to reinvent itself and compete with its American cousin. In all probability though, even if Shirley and his brothers had stepped aside we would be talking now about some other major organisation that took over British wrestling after them and lost a load of money. There wasn't the cash or the forward thinking to compete with the American bandwagon, which turned the eye of the British wrestling fan who forgot all about the oriental in the mask, or the fat men in spandex. And when the life support machine was finally switched off, and wrestling was allowed to die nobody cared anymore anyway.

Across the country, the CD was replacing vinyl and tape as the 1980s wore on. In a similar fashion, people now called for American heroes like Hulk Hogan and the Ultimate Warrior to strut their stuff, their veins throbbing with anabolic steroids.

Nobody wanted the chip-fat, kiss-me-quick hat world of British wrestling after 1986. There was no more wrestling at the dilapidated Grand Ballroom, with its nicotine-stained baths, shit-stained walls and cracked sinks. Gone were the smoky nights of theatrics, broken limbs, and buckets full of spit and blood on the apron, as it all skidded towards the end of the line.

To say that Max was a shrewd businessman would probably be an understatement but, in the true tradition of those that had gone before him, Joint Promotions was run on a shoestring, and this was why they could monopolise for as long as they did. They did good business and they paid the wrestlers a pittance, but then some of them would have done it just to get on TV. Some of the big names were visited by tax inspectors who thought they were on the fiddle; they were famous so they had to be rich, right? The inspectors could not believe it when they realised the pittance they were being paid.

When the wrestlers travelled they were given a £2 a night allowance which didn't go far, and as for the digs, Banger remembers Max putting them all up above a transport café. Imagine the looks the punters gave them next morning as they came in to get their breakfast and saw Giant Haystacks, Banger Walsh, and Jackie Turpin all sat there eating egg and chips.

Max never let any of them top up their money by selling their own signed photographs, and many of the wrestlers had to break their balls by doing a day job as well. They were all household names, but none of them had two pennies to rub together, and by the mid-1980s the writing was very much on the wall for British wrestling, although many chose to ignore it for a while longer.

In his 1985 autobiography, Jackie Pallo mentioned that wrestling was fixed, but it was Banger Walsh's exposé which made the front page of *The Sun* newspaper on 18 February and this really hammered home one of the last nails, and he was not a popular man. Most of the wrestling community turned against him, and in retrospect he says that he regrets what he did. It was just one in a series of events that killed the business off, and when he was approached by a reporter and offered a lot of money to tell his story that is what he did.

Other factors played a part, not even the big promoters in England could compete with Sky TV, and when wrestling started to get moved around to different time slots on terrestrial TV, it lost some of its following, although it was still pulling in millions of viewers.

After years in the wilderness, Brian Dixon's All-Star Promotions were seriously challenging Joint for supremacy, then *World of*

Sport was taken off the TV in September 1985, and Dickie Davies was no more. In an interview, Mick McManus said he knew that the writing had been on the wall for a number of years, but it had taken longer to come to an end than he had expected. The rot had set in in the late 1970s, and he blamed fighters like Haystacks and Daddy. For big men, he thought they did the very best they could, and he was careful not to label them as poor wrestlers.

Just like Dickie Davies's ever more exuberant moustaches, the wrestling itself became a farce. The technicality and skill were lost to the notion of total entertainment between a big sweaty man, and another big sweaty man with lots of hair. These were the days of the super-heavyweights and for poor old Mick, who stood at 5ft 6in and weighed 12.5st, there was no way he could tangle with big buggers like these, and this put him at a disadvantage straight away.

Live Aid happened during the summer of 1985, and it was watched by an estimated 1.9 billion people worldwide. At the same time, wrestling was bouncing around the TV schedule, and it was a massive blow to the business. Joint Promotions were expecting a straightforward renewal of their TV contract, but they found they now had to share with All-Star on a rotation basis. The business was beginning to implode, and there was a backlash against Banger's article, which also gave details about wages and other private details.

The first WrestleMania happened on 31 March in New York's Madison Square Garden, and all of these things contributed to what was to come. The relationship between Banger and the Crabtrees had been destroyed, and this led to Banger offering Daddy a "proper fight" through *The Sun* which never came about; it was typical tabloid shenanigans.

If Greg Dyke had been looking for ammunition to axe the ageing dinosaur TV wrestling had become, he must have felt like a dog with two dicks when the answer dropped straight through his letterbox with the Betterware catalogue one morning. He was quick to realise it was coming to the end of a one-way street despite the following it still had. It didn't help when the illusion was shattered, and then nobody knew whether to take wrestling seriously as a sport, or as straightforward entertainment. Whatever it was, it was no longer appealing to the kids with their new Commodore Amigas and their satellite TV. For that reason, the axe began to fall, but Shirley would continue to perform in the ring to the grotesque end which came about in 1993 when he was but a shadow of his former self.

Things did continue as normal for a while, although Banger Walsh never wrestled again. Shirley carried on with personal and TV appearances, although awkward questions about wrestling and the newspapers were never allowed to be asked. On FA Cup Final day there was always a massive audience so Max booked him in to tag with Mick McMichael, and they went through the motions against Peter Lapaque and Tommy Lorne. One night Banger's wife Carol got a phone call from a woman called Elena, and she told her she had a seven-year-old son by her husband. Putting the call on loud speaker, Banger recognised the voice straight away. It was Eunice trying to stir up trouble because of the article he had done for *The Sun*, but this time she failed.

There was so much crazy stuff going on back then and Shirley didn't know the half of it. He was busy with things like the Daddies Sauce commercials, and any money he did make went straight to Eunice for safekeeping. At the beginning of the year, he was asked to appear at the Pooh Bear Reading Assistance Society in Hull, and these were the type of events in which he went down really well with the children. Unfortunately, he was fighting with Danny Collins against Drew McDonald and Sid Cooper in Ashford, Kent, so he was unable to attend. Despite everything Shirley was trying to do, a corner had been turned and, after eight years in the limelight his star began to fade, but he wasn't the one who was desperate to hold on to it.

> *"What will be, will be, all things have their day, and all things must pass. I had a wonderful time as Big Daddy*

and when it was all over it left me kind of flat I'll admit. All the times I'd been tired and wished it would all come to an end, when it did I was left at a loose end. When all the horrible things were going on in the papers, it did affect things but the fans still turned up to see Big Daddy of course, but wrestling was changing. We underestimated the influence American wrestling would have, and as soon as it arrived in Britain, there was no way we could compete. Brian Dixon carried on with wrestling shows just as Max did, but he reverted to the American style and took his shows around the holiday camps and made quite a success of it."

Approaching 55, Shirley had neither the will nor strength to fight the waves of anger that were being directed towards the Crabtrees when the TV went pear-shaped. The age of innocence was over, they'd had a good run, and that was that. Journalists started to dig deeper into Shirley's past and, with such a loose cannon as a wife, it was hard to keep going.

With Jane, he would sometimes take cover and lay low from the world for a while. Spending time together just chilling out as father and daughter, watching films or walking on the moors and out of the way was a real release. More and more Shirley felt like jacking it in, but the show had to go on and Max hadn't been beaten just yet. In *The Sun*, an article written by Piers Morgan and David Croft titled "Big Daddy bottles it" appeared about the proposed fight with Banger Walsh, as all sorts of things started to emerge and most of it was rubbish.

Stories about wrestlers cutting themselves for an extra fiver, and other things just as damaging, but of course this was nothing to do with Shirley, he was simply on the payroll even if his brother was in charge. He was the figurehead in the line of sight as all the Crabtree boys were lumped together and blamed for the demise of the wrestling which had once been an integral part of Saturday afternoons.

There was a feeling that the public had been cheated to some degree, and even when wrestlers like Mick McManus and Rollerball Rocco were interviewed on TV, they would not openly admit that it was fixed. Everybody was now grabbing what they could but in truth Shirley did not panic, it was Max that did that as things gradually started to slip from his grasp, and a final throw of the dice was sought.

Chapter Seventeen
The Death Of Malcolm Kirk

B Y THE beginning of 1986, things were starting to calm down a little for Greg Dyke who had axed *World of Sport* the previous September, which had made him deeply unpopular. He was half-expecting a visit from Giant Haystacks who told the press what he would like to do to the man who would ultimately go on to stop TV wrestling altogether.

Greg needed to reinvent Saturday afternoons, but getting rid of the popular sports magazine show was something the public didn't like, and when he decided to swing the axe and drop wrestling from the schedule not only were the fans and wrestlers up in arms, but it also spelled the end for what had been a major British pastime. Once upon a time crystal sets, Tommy Handley and alchemy had been popular, but all of those things had been surpassed. Eventually, Greg was told he had to drop one sport, and having to choose between wrestling, darts, and snooker was easy for him.

He cringed at the thought of wrestling's image so there really was no contest. The fact that wrestling had its ass ripped out and had been branded "fake" didn't help either, and was of course a different image to the professional, legitimate image ITV was trying to portray, even though it could still draw in good viewing figures for a while.

We must remember that ITV only had one channel then, and something with such a following today would probably end up on one of ITV's other channels, or be banished to Channel Five with Aussie soap operas *Neighbours* and *Home and Away*. It would have in all likelihood still been on TV, although it may well have been tucked away somewhere on some obscure satellite channel late at night. Specialist viewing stuck between a channel which constantly showed re-runs of *Tenko* and *Wagon Train*, and one watched mainly by single gentlemen intent on giving their wrist muscles a workout.

It would also have had to change its image if it had have competed with American wrestling, and perhaps an organisation such as Brian Dixon's All-Star may have taken over and replaced the wet Wednesday evening on Blackpool Pier feel the sport had under Joint Promotions.

In truth, Shirley had done his time, and should have taken it on the chin alongside his brothers. He should have spent more time sat in his paddling pool, or walking on the moors with the dog, rather than helping his brother as he tried to remain in control.

Max was determined to fight, and his efforts stepped up a gear. At first, he was fighting for his slice of the TV action, and when that went he continued to run shows all over the country, believing there was still a future for him and British wrestling on the box. With his brother soldiering on the best he could in the latter part of the 1980s and early 1990s, perhaps a few people came to see Big Daddy for more morbid reasons.

Keeping him at the top as the only major star meant the other really big names around at the time were from the same generation. Max had not created others to fill Shirley's place, such was his desire to remain in total control. It was in America where tag teams such as the British Bulldogs gained their fame, while working for Joint (which became Ring Wrestling Stars in the last couple of years of Max's involvement) they were just part of the supporting cast. For all of his business acumen and creative flair, this fatal mistake seems almost neurotically short-sighted. Did he not see his brother heaving his guts up night after night in the ring as he struggled for breath?

He was unwilling to push youngsters through, and for any institution or sport to continue there must always be the up-and-coming apprentices. The Daddy formula was still working, still pulling in the crowds, although looking at Shirley's performances it was clear that he had lost his aggressive edge. The fact that he spent the day before his 56th birthday in Harrogate recording a televised fight indicates that he wasn't slowing down either.

He did have his actual birthday off, before appearing in King's Lynn the next day which wasn't much of a break for a bloke staring 60 in the face. Between his birthday on 14 November and Christmas, he did another 28 shows all over the country which would all take their toll on him in the end. Why did he feel the need to work himself to death?

We have discussed many of these elements in previous chapters of course. Shirley was a proud man, a follower of the old-school work-until-you-drop methodology, and the image of his mother carrying all of those bags of coal up the stairs stayed with him and pushed him onwards. If she had done it so would he. They were a family no matter what differences they all had; they must not run out on each other; they would learn from the mistakes their father had made. Mistakes he had apologised for on his death bed when the boys had tried to give him words of comfort.

All the anger subsided only when he was dying, even the fact that the Lord had seen fit to give him a longer life than their mother (who had died at the beginning of the 1970s) all flowed under the bridge of life and into the waters of death and the abyss beyond. It was a funny old world which was constantly changing. In the blink of an eye, those that were in the middle running of things could vanish without a trace.

ITVs 1986 Christmas wrestling coverage was shown on 27 December, and it was the match Shirley had recorded at Harrogate on his birthday. Teaming up with Richie Brooks and Roy Regal, they scored a knockout victory against Haystacks, Sid Cooper, and Charles McGee, in what was Shirley's last televised match until April 1987. It was also the year of the Fergusons as Sarah married

Prince Andrew, and Alex (no relation) became the manager of Manchester United. There was also Diego Maradona's infamous hand of God incident against England at the 1986 World Cup in Mexico, and of course, the return of Kendo Nagasaki, appearing in a ladder match at the London Hippodrome at Christmas 1986.

Comparing him, or other British fighters of that generation active at the time, to the pieces of American meat such as Hulk Hogan, Randy Savage, and the Ultimate Warrior, was a silly thing to do. There was no contest for the ever-increasing number of Brits tuning in to the benefits of Sky TV and the high-octane world of the WWF.

Sick of people stealing his act, Kendo slipped once again into the mask and cape and went back to work. Granted his work clothes weren't the sort of thing you would hang about on street corners in, but if anyone was going to earn it was going to be the original, Peter Thornley.

The year also stands as a marker as it was the last of Shirley's "golden years" as Big Daddy, even though he did continue for a while yet. His output in the ring had certainly nosedived, but he still entertained the crowd as best he could, realising that he only had to do one of two moves to get the crowd going. Liverpool beat Everton 3-1 on FA Cup Final day as Daddy was wheeled out once again for the cameras as the whole business wobbled under the weight of the super-heavyweights it was trying to support.

Despite all of this the crowds still came, and if Daddy wasn't on the bill the show had less of a chance of selling out. The following year was destined to be much darker for Shirley, not just because the business was tumbling out of control, but because of a tragedy in the ring. Things changed forever for him, and if he could have changed the situation he would have. The truth is he was trapped, and the two main forces in his life needed him to remain as Big Daddy.

Being stuck between Eunice and Max was hard work and he retreated whenever he had the chance. He would just get in the car and drive away from them for a bit of peace and quiet. At this point in his life it was perhaps only with Jane that he shared a common cause, and if he hadn't have had that he would have been in trouble. It was when he suddenly realised he had caused harm himself, and things were irreversible, that the change within him occurred.

The past will always be the past it will never be the same again, but death makes things even worse. He had grieved before of course, but for somebody to die because of him was something he never really got over, and he continued to think and have nightmares about this until his last days.

He did mention Kirk on his death bed, and he hoped that God wasn't going to hold it against him on the day of reckoning. Those that were waiting to see morbidity were soon to be entertained, but it was not Shirley who would drop dead in the ring. In time, he did begin to listen, and let go of what were once the most glorious days of his life, but he was not the only one taking a risk with his life in the ring. There were others out there risking heart attack and stroke and Shirley was absolutely distraught at the thought of killing Malcolm Kirk when a move he was doing went wrong.

Malcolm Kirk was a big man, a big bald man, who became Kojak Kirk after Telly Savalas's TV character, and then King Kong Kirk, although he wrestled under other guises. Many of the old wrestlers called him "Mucky", as in "Mucky Mal Kirk", another gimmick, from another time, in an era that cannot return just like the dear man himself. Born in Featherstone, which is 25 miles from Halifax, Kirk was six years younger than Shirley, although they had similar rugby league upbringings having both played for professional clubs as youngsters. Weighing around 24st and standing at 6ft 1in there wasn't a great deal of difference between Shirley and Kirk apart from the fact that Kirk played the bad guy, or villain if we use proper wrestling talk.

Kirk died on Sunday 24 August 1987 at the Hippodrome Circus in Great Yarmouth. Andy Harris, who was in the crowd at the time, remembers that Daddy was teamed with his nephew Greg Valentine against King Kong Kirk and King Kendo (played by Bill Clarke). Everything was going along as normal until the Big Daddy splash from which Mal failed to get up. There was a look of shock and bewilderment on Shirley's face once it dawned on him that something serious had happened, and then the backroom lads lifted him out on a stretcher and away.

A doctor came out of the crowd and did what he could, and Mal was still alive at that point fighting for life. There was chaos ringside with people worrying what had happened to him, and the front of house manager was walking around the ring in a daze. After Daddy had splashed Kirk, the ref counted him out and witnesses say it took Shirley a few seconds to realise there was a problem. When he didn't get up they say they could see the look of rising panic in his face as he looked away from the crowd with whom he was celebrating victory.

The rest of the programme continued but at the end of the night they were informed Mal had died, and a minute's silence occurred the following week as the wrestling world mourned one of their own.

Destined to travel to America to carve out a new career, Mal was 52 years old when he died. Usually, during a Daddy splash-down, Shirley's weight was transferred into the ground and not into the opponent, but when he did the move on Mal it went wrong. All of his weight hit him square in the chest and he suffered a massive heart attack and died. Sometimes this did happen, but on this occasion it proved fatal because Mal had a problem with his heart that nobody had picked up on before.

His widow Ilona was grief-stricken and then she got angry and ended up doing a piece on her late husband for the newspapers. She told the world how he had hated wrestling, and that he had lost his life for £30 a night which was what he earned. There had been a meeting with Max after he had died and he gave her some money which he said she could keep if she did not go to the press but she told him where to stick it. A night of wrestling was organised and all of the proceeds went straight to Ilona and the family without any conditions at all, and thus the divide between the Crabtrees and many of the wrestlers expanded even further.

There was almost a mob mentality brewing as disaster after disaster brought the business to its knees clutching its balls. The fun and frivolity of those man in glorious red, blue, and gold spandex had now lost its innocence as an era shuddered to an end and rusted into the ground. All that is left today is a collection of photos and posters, and a bunch of former wrestlers, most of pensionable age. They meet every year at the reunions and lace stories of famous matches with tales about hip replacements, heart bypasses and death. Like moths to candles was their relationship with the TV camera, and despite the state many of them find themselves in today there was no financial recompense.

The tabloids ran many stories on how Shirley had been affected by Kirk's death and there was a lot of bitterness not just towards him, but towards Max and the business itself. Shirley was cleared of any charges over Kirk's death, but this was truly the blackest moment in his career. Grief made many people speak out against the Crabtrees and Joint Promotions, which Max had bought outright in 1986. Many of the things that were said were true but the wages had always been low, and wrestlers knew they were never going to topple Shirley while his brother was in control so nothing new was really mentioned, just announced to the general public.

And after the mysteries had been pointed out the British scene was discarded and left in a draw somewhere like an old mobile phone that had been upgraded. What everybody was unanimous about was the sad fact that a wrestler had died for not a great deal of money at all, but the health and safety regulations many of us spit at today were not in place at the time.

Take, for example, both Shirley and Kirk's body mass index and of course, the strain carrying such weight must have had on the heart. Shirley's diet was high-protein with milk, butter, eggs and high-cholesterol foods all washed down with a full English breakfast full of saturated fat. Would men as old as they were be granted the necessary licence they would surely need to wrestle in 2013?

There is also the issue of money, and even if Max had been blessed with a "giving gene" there would have needed to be major restructuring of the business if it was going to be fairer to the wrestlers. And even if there had been a wrestlers' union arguing out a pay deal, in the end it would have all been for nothing because it was all coming to an end.

> "I knocked him back into the corner then grabbed him and threw him across the ring. He came back at me and I hit him across the chest with a forearm smash. Kirk fell down and then I splashed on top of him. He struggled on the canvas but I held him for the count of three. That gave us the match. I stood up to the sound of fans. They gave me a six-minute ovation. It was total pandemonium with families and young children leaving their seats and rushing towards me to shake my hand. I did not see Mal Kirk until time had elapsed and when I managed to push my way back towards him he was still lying on the canvas. His face was purple and I realised he was in great distress. I immediately shouted 'quick, quick get an ambulance – quick'. I just could not believe it, and didn't know what to think. He was a very strong man, as strong as horses, and at least a couple of pounds heavier than me. I just could not take in what had happened… I still can't. One minute Mal was fighting a good hard match. The next minute he was on the floor with people around him offering help. I left the ring in a complete daze. People bundled me away, it was terrible. I didn't know what to think. We are professionals and we know that wrestling is a very, very tough game."

Amid a scene of total confusion and terror they had done their best to save Kirk, but it was not to be. His death served as a watershed but still the band played on as the ship sank.

Hard like the old man, that was the way the Crabtrees had been taught, and Max had more of his influence instilled in him than his two brothers. Their mother Marion had been very protective of her boys, and she would always do her best to sit down with them and share a bit of love and that perhaps rubbed off on Shirley more than the others. Max had that competitive money-making edge from early on, and many people say that is how you have to be in business if you wish to succeed. Today, there are still many people who speak badly of Max because of the way he treated people, and he must know, deep down, that this was so because he does not attend the reunions.

Although there are no outward stories about him being jealous of Shirley, he perhaps had enough of an attention-seeking personality to have exploited the fame more than Shirley because he did not shy away from the glare of the lights. Shirley loved being Big Daddy, but he didn't need to be him. If it had never have happened it wouldn't have made the blindest bit of difference – he would have carried on living his life in exactly the same way. As long as he had that tenner in his tracksuit pocket, and the wife wasn't drunk and causing problems, he was as happy as a sandboy.

After Kirk's death, Shirley made a call to Ilona and insisted on being alone when he did so. He told his family that she had thanked him for calling. There was even a photo of both taken together at the inquest and Shirley desperately wanted Ilona not to blame him otherwise he would have told the photographer to leave out taking such a photo at such a sensitive time. Again, that feeling of loneliness that welled within him needed to be made secure. He may not have needed fame, but he did need to feel like he was loved or else it wouldn't be worth going on. Living with the knowledge that he had caused somebody's death, even unintentionally, was not an easy thing to wake up to each morning, but more tragic than that was the fact that Mal's daughter Natasha would grow up without ever knowing her father.

There were those who went too far, and there were those who were angry with Shirley at the time, but in the end, it was just a tragic accident and should have been the sign for the Crabtrees to jack it all in.

Being pissed off with the business and the brothers was one thing, but there were those who somehow implied that they were responsible for Mal's death collectively and this is not so. Maybe Joint Promotions worked people to death for a pittance, and maybe Shirley had been responsible for Mal's death. At the end of the day every single man makes his own decisions and any one of them could have made that fatal move, or received that killer blow, and they knew this only too well.

As the 1980s moved on towards its completion, Shirley looked more and more out of place in the ring. It was like the stuffing had been knocked out of him, but he wasn't done just yet. He was still going in 1988, the year of Bros-mania, chinos, and Grolsch bottle tops being worn on people's boots and being held up as fashion.

Around this time, Premier Promotions was started by a chap called John Freemantle, and they started to present a more punishing version of British wrestling as the crown slipped further. None of this would make Shirley ease back on his schedule, in fact, it was just the opposite and in the end, he would pay the consequences. When he reached his 60th birthday in 1990, he had fought in so many matches already that year, which was crazy for a man of his age. He didn't even let up after Mal's death, fighting the next night in Bridlington, then Llandudno and Southport before taking a couple of days off.

The last televised wrestling bout for Shirley was recorded on 26 November 1988 and shown on TV 16 days later. In what was billed as a novelty spectacular he teamed up with Tom Thumb and Kashmir Singh against Task Force Three for Dale and Martins Promotions in Rickmansworth. There was one more show shown on TV a week later, a "transatlantic spectacular" featuring WWF fighters, and then that was it. Kent Walton presented *Final Bell* on 17 December 1988, and looked back at the past 33 years and all the fantastic characters that had appeared before the credits rolled. British wrestling ended for good on terrestrial television.

Still, there were feuds, new ones with Fit Finlay and Drew McDonald, for Daddy who was teaming up with up-and-coming stars such as Sammy Lee, Dynamite Kid, Young David, Roy Regal, and Chris Adams and this was about as near as these new lads would get to becoming top of a bill Shirley was appearing on.

Early in 1988, Kendo Nagasaki and Rollerball Rocco's tag partnership fell apart, and they feuded violently for a couple of years after the TV had finished, but it had all been seen before. The only new thing was Steve Grey, who won the first of four European lightweight titles that year, but yet another blow came about in 1989 when Wayne Bridges decided to retire.

Since the wrestling had finished on TV, Max had recovered from the shock by furiously plotting a way back in. In the end he and Shirley made a last-ditch effort to get their shows on Sky TV, pointing out WWF's popularity as a tool to convince the head of programming that their shows would be popular. Unfortunately, the chap was Australian, and he had never heard of Big Daddy. He was also only offering £500 a show so a deal was never made. The Crabtrees' dominance of British wrestling was over, and Max went back to his roots and started to promote small independent shows of his own, although he never ventured into the US style like some.

Jackie Pallo began promoting an American version of wrestling in the UK in 1990 as the old ways were washed away. This was the lowest point for British wrestling as the original stars retired and were almost completely forgotten by the tidal wave from the States, which seemed to delete all memory of what had occurred before. Up and down the country, in halls and theatres that smelled of sweat and liniment, there had been furious activity every night of the week. Now this had come to an end; the times had changed forever as more and more American tribute shows began to start up and sadly abandoned a British identity which had been in place for generations.

Chapter Eighteen

He Was The Daddy

THE FAST-FOOD chain McDonald's had expanded as far as Moscow by January 1990, although the Cold War was still going on. A tepid cup of tea or a cold Big Mac had the Russians up in arms but not as much as what was going on in Azerbaijan. Trouble started early in the year when Soviet troops occupied the region and killed 130 people.

Back home there was terrible news for author Salman Rushdie, who angered many Muslims with his book *The Satanic Verses*. Many thought it was blasphemous, and it incensed Ayatollah Khomeini so much that he issued a fatwa against him.

Around this time, Shirley was travelling with British cruiser-weight champion Ray Robinson. Trained by Cyril Knowles in the 1960s, they could always rely on him to put on a good hard match, and he was one of the few wrestlers they could still rely on to turn up week in, week out. Ray used to wrestle after Shirley had finished his match and even at this point in his career Ray recalls how the name Big Daddy needed to be on the bill if the night had any chance of selling enough tickets, which was getting harder and harder to do.

One night after a show in Buxton attracted a poor crowd Shirley lost his cool because he believed it hadn't been advertised properly, and not enough posters put up about the town. MC and referee Gordon Prior was there that night, and he remembers the incident quite clearly. The Crabtree lads were definitely feeling the strain at the time, and Shirley accused them all of wanting the limelight but not wanting to graft.

It was another sign that the good days were gone, although Daddy also had a monthly comic running for a time as he continued to earn himself a wage in England. Martin Ruane would try his luck in America, eventually leaving Giant Haystacks behind him and enjoying a brief moment in the spotlight fighting as Loch Ness before his death.

Forever the meek and modest man, Gordon Prior remembers that Shirley liked to be introduced simply as "people's hero Big Daddy" rather than grander introductions such as "star of TV show *This Is Your Life*" or "former Blackpool lifeguard Big Daddy".

Nice and simple was the way, you always knew where you were with Shirley, and he was what you would call dependable. He was also an inspiration to a lot of people, even helping Ray Robinson, who was struggling with his fitness so Shirley could advise him despite his rather portly physique at the time. He told him how he and his brothers would drive their mum mad when they were kids by constantly rolling about the front room for an hour or two at night bumping off walls and trying not to smash anything.

Ray tried this and after a while he wasn't feeling so tired out come the end of the fight as his stamina improved, although his wife would have found it difficult to see Rolf Harris on TV as he presented *Animal Hospital*. Over the years, Ray has heard a lot of people slag Shirley off but one thing he is sure of is that nobody would do it to his face.

"The wrestling business is very fickle, and you sometimes have to be a hypocrite to keep everyone happy. It's all part of the charade, all part of the performance, and your true friends are the ones you keep in touch with when you're no longer wrestling. I kept in touch with a few when I packed it in as Big Daddy, not many, but just a couple of people I went

218

back a long way with. My brothers were the same when it all ended, I don't think any of us wanted much fuss. They were good days, golden times and I feel very fortunate to have been such a big part of the wrestling scene during the seventies and eighties. I know there are those that criticise me, criticise my brother for the way he ran the business but Max is his own man at the end of the day, and I had nothing to do with that side of things. Obviously, we were all in it together but when we went home it wasn't like the Waltons or anything like that I can assure you. We had our own lives outside of the wrestling world."

Shirley did around 200 more shows in 1992 all across the country, and his schedule was pretty relentless until something happened that stopped him in his tracks for a time. One night after a show he was sitting in the back of the car, and Max noticed he couldn't hold up a cup of tea; his hands shook, and he spilt it into his lap. It was then that they knew that something serious had happened; he had received a bang to the head during the fight which had brought on Bell's palsy, a dysfunction of the cranial nerve in the face. Typically, it causes a kind of facial paralysis and can lead to brain tumours and strokes, and this was the start of the road that would ultimately lead to Shirley's death.

Treatment using corticosteroids helped, and Jane helped teach him how to use the facial muscles, to a degree, so he returned to some sort of normality. When we look at pictures of Shirley in his later years, we can see that one side of his face has dropped, but still he went on for a while longer.

In 1993, he kept the same punishing schedule, even tagging up with Steve Grey in Midhurst on his birthday against Count Von Zuppi and Sid Cooper. Despite how much Jane pleaded with him to quit it fell on deaf ears, but deep down inside he must have known the damage he was doing to himself. However, the doctors passed him fit, and he continued into the 1990s with hardly any let-up. Towards the end of 1992, as he was recovering from Bell's, he slowed things down for a time, but he did not stop. Once he thought he had made a full recovery he pushed on into 1993, and he continued to do four, five, sometimes six shows a week.

In the end, Jane had to grab hold of him by the arms. Full of tears she yelled at him "stop!" She screamed, she cried and when she looked at him it was like looking into the eyes of a frightened child. He knew once it all ended he would be redundant, without a purpose, spending his days driving in his old Lada to Blackpool for a swim, or pottering about the house or doing the crossword.

Shirley's last bout was in Margate on 29 December 1993, and it was an end to a career which had started 46 years earlier as an amateur which was a truly remarkable feat. He did not know how to do anything else, and once he quit Eunice and Max treated him accordingly. What was even sadder was the fact that he knew that he was now "redundant" and in the end, he sunk into a sort of depression from which visits to the only daughter he had ever really known provided respite.

The WWF show SummerSlam drew a crowd of 80,000 to Wembley in 1992, but still Max continued to make a wage with his Ring Wrestling Stars. For a while after Shirley had retired he thought he was on the way back. When the British Bulldogs, Davey Boy Smith and Dynamite Kid, returned from America and started to work for him again he was chuffed to bits, but it wasn't to last. Brian Dixon's All-Star promotions had also been doing very well after the TV finished thanks largely to Kendo Nagasaki, but the boom had worn off by 1993, and Kendo decided to retire once again as All-Star became established on the holiday camp circuit.

On Sky, the WWF shows had been given the old Saturday afternoon *World of Sport* time slot, but when the Bulldogs were lured back across the pond, Max decided to jack it in for good, and he ran his last shows in 1995. The first National Lottery draw took place a few days after Shirley's 64th birthday in November 1994, and the family hit the town to celebrate a new beginning. It was to be one of the last memories Jane has of going out with her dad for the evening, and they really enjoyed themselves.

Eunice behaved herself and Jane bought him a lottery ticket, and he won £84 so it was all smiles for a time, but they hid a deep fear. Psychologists talk of Eros, the life instinct, and Thanatos the death instinct and as each ability and tool was taken away from Shirley, the deeper he sank. A minor stroke crippled him further, and this was the beginning of a series of such episodes which would gradually take away his mobility and his freedom. Once he could no longer drive he was unable to escape from Eunice and her crazy lifestyle; and that would signal the end.

While he was ill, a damaging article appeared in the paper by his stepdaughter Linda, and it really hurt. In an article titled "Big Daddy's a Big Baddy at Home" which was printed in the *News of the World* on Sunday 30 January 1994, she told how he forced her mother to live in fear in the kitchen. There was no mention of her having bottles of drink secreted in places like the oven and the tumble dryer, and there was no mention of Eunice's pissed-up psychotic behaviour which had at its worst ended up with her waking up on the floor somewhere having been robbed, or spending all the money Shirley earned. There was no mention of what she had put in the babies' bottle, or any of the other things Shirley, Paul and Jane had to endure on a weekly basis.

Under Linda's picture was the word "angry", but in truth, she had been this way ever since Shirley had entered her life. She blamed him for the split between her mother and her real father Arthur Wright, and she failed to recall his alcohol-fuelled abuses. Distressed when she recalls her father's final years of life, Jane remembers that there was still no peace for him even though he was ill. Shortly after he had the first stroke in 1994, she got a call from Halifax Police Station telling her that Shirley had been arrested. When she went to pick him up it turned out that Eunice had hit him over the head with a baseball bat, and he was in a hell of a state. He got into Jane's car but refused to stay at her house, choosing instead to return home.

221

Despite being pregnant, Jane spent as much time as she could with her dad, making sure he built up the use of his legs as much as possible with regular visits to the physiotherapist, and the osteopath near to where she worked as a hairdresser. She tried as best she could to make him feel good about himself. The fact that he was still able to drive kept him sane and was one of the few things stopping him from sinking into a full state of depression.

Shirley was the sort of man who wouldn't have gone to the doctor for such a "psychological" complaint, and one time when Jane went to visit she found him sat in the front room in the dark on his own. With his facial droop, he looked a shadow of his former self, and when she asked him if he was alright and put her arms around him, he just cried like a baby and said: "Look at the state of me, I'm fucked." Training and fresh air were his life, and he still did it every day until it eventually became too much for him. It was a terrible thing to happen to such a man, and he never could understand how some people who had smoked and drank all of their lives managed to still be going in their 90s without any problems at all.

More and more Shirley was beginning to depend on his family, and he spent the last couple of years driving about and visiting people. He needed that escape but one evening when he was leaving Jane's in his Lada his lack of control and co-ordination led to him damaging the car and a bed of roses before he screeched up the street. Jane recalls that this signalled the beginning of the end for him, she was forced to take the car keys off of him, and he looked like a condemned man.

By then he could hardly walk, and shuffled along. Eunice even got him a Zimmer frame as his mobility deserted him. Unfortunately, Max was nowhere to be seen during these dark days. Shirley would turn up at the farm but there was no purpose in him coming. Whether the brotherly bond had been severed and broken during those latter years, who can tell? One thing for sure is that Max was still chasing the money, but it wouldn't have hurt for him to be involved in his brother's life a bit more. They had been brothers and friends right from the start, before Brian had been born when their old man had left.

They had been through all the trials and tribulations of life together, and it is sad to think this closeness was non-existent come the end. When Shirley was no longer capable of going up to the farm, Max did not take this as a cue to start regularly visiting his brother and to help out Eunice.

In September 1997, Jane received a call at work telling her that Shirley had suffered a massive stroke, and she left immediately for the hospital. Shirley had woken up in the morning in a state of confusion, calling Eunice "Marion", his mother's name. He was talking gibberish and using the wrong words so Eunice called for the ambulance. To add insult to injury Shirley had to be carried out of bed by several firemen and down the steep steps and stairs of the cottage to the waiting ambulance.

In the hospital ward, he had a look of confusion and panic on his face, which lit up as soon as Jane arrived, and they sat together and shared a quiet moment until their peace was shattered by Eunice's voice. After the firemen had taken Shirley away she had decided to get drunk before she turned up at the hospital to see what was going on. The next thing they knew she had flung the curtains back and started shouting: "Come on Shirley, there's a taxi outside, we're going home."

There was no way Shirley could have left; he was paralysed down one side of his body, but still she persisted. By now, everyone was staring so Jane slapped her across the face and told her to leave.

Unfortunately, Shirley's condition worsened and he started to have a series of fits, which meant he was then bedridden but, despite the confusion, Jane says his mind was intact, and he was fully aware of what was going on. With each fit, there was more damage and near the end, when he was having a massive fit in front of Jane, Max walked in. He looked at Shirley, and then at Jane shuddering with fear, and he turned around and left without trying to comfort Jane, or take her out of the room.

Shortly after this Shirley suffered a massive stroke and because of the strength of his body, he battled on for another eight weeks, but he finally passed away on 2 December 1997 at Halifax General Hospital.

> *"One day we will be forgotten. We had our time but life moves on; it flows like a river never stopping for anything at all… People have given me more love than any human being is entitled to and for that I am truly grateful."*